Research and Publication Ethics

About the Authors

Dr. Debabrata Basu is presently serving as Professor in the Department of Agricultural Extension, Bidhan Chandra Krishi Viswavidyalaya, West Bengal. He was former professor of Agricultural Extension in Visva-Bharati Sriniketan (2009-11). Dr. Basu has 28 years of teaching and research experience in the field of agricultural extension, rural sociology, rural development with specialization in adult and distance learning (IGNOU). Professor Basu has written twenty text books, reference books, and manuals for undergraduate and post graduate students. He has authored 95 research articles in national and international journals of repute. He got awards and fellowship for his contribution from academic societies. His areas of research cover research methodology, social network analysis, extension education, adult and continuing education, gender studies and agriculture, participatory development, Agricultural market research, indigenous technical knowledge system, readability of language, community based disaster management and other allied areas of extension science.

E-mail address: drdbasu@gmail.com

Dr. Samarpan Chakraborty is currently working as Subject Matter Specialist Agricultural Extension (Gr. A) at Dhaanyaganga Krishi Vigyan Kemdra (ICAR-KVK Murshidabad Additional) in the aegis of RKMVERI, Belur, WB. He had his Doctoral Degree in Agricultural Extension from BCKV as a UGC Research Fellow. He has qualified in the National Eligibility Test for Assistant Professor conducted by UGC in his maiden attempt. He has received his M.Sc. (Ag) from BCKV as the First Class First in the university and received Governor's Gold medal for this achievement. He has obtained his Graduation in Agricultural Sciences (B.Sc. Agriculture) from Palli Sikhsha Bhavana, VISVA BHARATI as the First Class Second in the University and secured overall 9th rank in the All India Entrance Examination for post-graduation conducted by ICAR. His Research areas covers the fields of Farmers suicide, off farm migration, Disillusionments of Indian Farmers, Social Network analysis etc.

E-mail address: samarpan.chakraborty92@gmail.com

Dr. Aditya Sinha is working as Assistant Professor-*cum*-Junior Scientist in the Department of Extension Education at Bihar Agricultural University, Sabour, Bihar, India, since 2012. He received his Ph.D. degree in Agricultural Extension from Bidhan Chandra Krishi Viswavidyalaya, WestBengal, in 2020; an M.Sc. degree in Extension Education from Banaras Hindu University, Varanasi, in 2011 and B.Sc. in Agriculture from Visva Bharati University, Santiniketan, India, in 2009. He has been awarded first prize in the best Ph.D. thesis award by MANAGE, Hyderabad for the year 2020. He has also received the best Ph.D. story award from the Department of Science and Technology, Government of India in 2019. He has worked as a summer intern in IIT Madras during his Masters and IIT Ropar during his Ph.D. He has worked on research projects on rural leadership, entrepreneurship and human-media interaction. He is passionate about educational technology and agricultural journalism.

E-mail address: inc.aditya@gmail.com

Research and Publication Ethics

A Textbook

Debabrata Basu
Samarpan Chakraborty
Aditya Sinha

CONCEPT PUBLISHING COMPANY PVT. LTD.
NEW DELHI-110059

ISBN: 978-93-5439-084-5 (HB)
ISBN: 978-93-5439-085-2 (PB)

First Published 2022

Published and Printed by

Concept Since 1974

Concept Publishing Company Pvt. Ltd.
A/15-16, Commercial Block, Mohan Garden
New Delhi-110059 (India)
T: +91-11-41101460
E: publishing@conceptpub.com, W: www.conceptpub.com

Cataloging in Publication Data–Courtesy: D.K. Agencies (P) Ltd. <docinfo@dkagencies.com>

Basu, D. (Debabrata), author.
Research and publication ethics : a textbook / Debabrata Basu, Samarpan Chakraborty, Aditya Sinha
pages cm
Includes bibliographical references and index
ISBN 9789354390845 (HB)
ISBN 9789354390852 (PB)

1. Research--Moral and ethical aspects. 2. Publishers and publishing--Moral and ethical aspects. I. Chakraborty, Samarpan, author. II. Sinha, Aditya (Assistant professor of extension education), author. III. Title.

LCC Q180.55.M67B37 2022 | DDC 174.95 23

Preface

Ethics, the fundamental to man's innate nature, should be the central force of the multifarious dimensions of a human being. But in this era of "Stress and Conflicts", the aspects of ethical living are being subdued drastically. Inclusion of morality, human values and ethics either formally or informally in their daily life can be the panacea for them. So, in the education system the learning of value and ethics is the need of the hour.

Higher Education and Research start with questions for which a researcher wishes to seek answers. Each of the aspects of research requires adherence to some basic ethical practices.

Publication is the other face of the research. Whatsoever a researcher reveals through his or her research is published for the knowing of the rest of the world about that. It is the basic responsibility of that researcher to maintain ethical standards for the benefits of the society.

This textbook on *Human Values and Ethics* has been written according to the syllabus recommended by the Experts Committee constituted by UGC. The restructured course curriculum has laid emphasis on the inclusion of ethics in Research and subsequent publication to enable the students to acquire personal skills, morality, values and ethics in their life.

In this book we have covered the whole syllabus and also added some more useful aspects related to this field, which will serve the purposes of the students of streams other than agriculture, horticulture and agricultural engineering like medical, pharmacy, social science, engineering and other professional courses. A common man will also feel interested with this book as it covers the general life aspects of human values and ethics.

The book is divided into six chapters covering the areas like— Philosophy and Ethics, Professional Ethics and Scientific Conduct, Research and Publication Ethics, Open Access Publishing, Publication Misconduct, Database and Research Metrics. The contents are presented in this book in an attractive and lucid way to make a convenient textbook for the students.

We hope this book will be of immense use for the students of different streams specially agriculture not only to obtain good marks but also to become a responsible citizen of the country.

Any suggestion for the betterment of this venture is highly appreciated.

2020 **Authors**

Contents

1

Philosophy and Ethics

"Philosophy is the first and the last Science." —*Aristotle*

1.0 Introduction to Philosophy

Philosophy is the mother of all arts and the true medicine of the mind, stated by Cicero. It is a persistent attempt to gain insight into the nature of the world and ourselves by systematic reflection. This field has emerged as a result of reflection over the experiences and problems of everyday living.

Aristotle considered philosophy as "the first and last science". The first science because it is logically presupposed by every other science, the last because it deals with reality in its ultimate principles and causes. He defines it as follows: "There is a science (that is Philosophy) which investigates being as being, and the attributes which belong to this in virtue of its own nature." We can find a gradual growth in the meaning of philosophy, as we go through the history of thought.

1.1 Origin of Philosophy

The term 'philosophy' has its roots in Greece and in Greek language. It is quite commonly known that *philosophia* etymologically means 'love of wisdom' (*Philia + Sophia*). But *sophia* had a much wider range of application than the modern English "wisdom". Wherever intelligence can be exercised—in practical affairs, in the mechanical arts, in business—there is room for *Sophia.*

The Greek historian Herodotus (484-424 B.C.) appears to have been the first to use the verb "to philosophize". As for the word "philosopher" (etymologically, a lover of wisdom), a certain somewhat unreliable tradition traces it back to Pythagoras (about 582-500 B.C.).

According to a tradition, Pythagoras was the first to describe himself as a philosopher. But both the words "philosopher" and "philosophy" are freely used in the writings of the disciples of Socrates (470-399 B.C.), and it is possible that he was the first to make use of them.

Herodotus used the verb *philosophein* in a context in which it means nothing more than the desire to find out. Pythagoras distinguished the *sophia* sought by the philosopher (knowledge based on contemplation) from the practical shrewdness of the businessman and the trained skills of the athlete.

Plato points to Socrates as *the* philosopher. Plato gives a few characteristics of philosophical wisdom, such as ability to enter into critical discussion, having direct access to "true reality", knowledge of the purpose of life etc.

1.2 Meaning of Philosophy

As evident from above, although philosophy is etymologically defined as 'love of wisdom', the meaning of wisdom is taken in a wider sense.

We will be dealing exclusively with the notion of wisdom.

Science can only tell us *how*, whereas philosophy can tell us *why*, things happen as they do. It is presumed here that science, inheriting the cosmological tradition, does not offer us the knowledge of ultimate reality; only philosophy can do this.

Although science too speaks about the *why* or the causes, the "general causes and principles" of the philosopher are "higher" and "more ultimate" than the causes and principles that science reveals to us.

There are two very different forms of activity now go under the name of "philosophy": one is essentially rational and critical, with logical analysis at its heart; the other is openly hostile to rational analysis to arrive at general conclusions by a phenomenological intuition or hermeneutical interpretation.

The various schools of thought, belonging to these two branches, make use of different procedures or methods, which will be taken up in another Unit.

Philosophy came to be thought of as running parallel to physics, the science of man as contrasted with the science of nature. Some of the later philosophers consider that the task of philosophy is to 'coordinate the most important general notions and fundamental principles of the various sciences.'

1.3 Concept of Philosophy

Philosophy is reflective knowledge. The sciences which are grouped together as philosophical are those in which we are forced back upon the problems of reflective thought, and cannot simply put them aside. The peculiar difficulties of reflective thought may account for the fact that these sciences are, more than others, a field in which we may expect to find disputes and differences of opinion. We need not be afraid that the whole field of human knowledge will come to be so divided up into special sciences that philosophy will disappear. The problems with which the philosopher occupies himself are real problems, which present themselves unavoidably to the thoughtful mind, and it is not convenient to divide these up among the several sciences.

It has been generally considered that philosophy is a purely abstract enterprise without any practical relevance. But as Marcel says, "philosophy has no weight and no interest whatever unless it sounds an echo in our life." Besides the traditionally accepted fields, philosophy brings to its embrace almost every other question. Everything is looked at in their ultimate causes and principles.

Today philosophy is brought down to philosophizing on questions with which the humans are constantly gripped. Thus it vibrates as a constant 'echo' in our life. This is what was done Socrates of old, and Kierkegaard of last century. In short, philosophy enables people to live a life of existential depth, moral integrity and religious conviction.

1.4 Definition of Philosophy

Oxford Dictionary defines 'philosophy' as that department of knowledge which deals with ultimate reality or with the most general causes and principles of things.

The Penguin Dictionary of Philosophy defines it as the study of the most fundamental and general concepts and principles involved in thought, action and reality.

Encyclopaedia of Philosophy defines philosophy as "Love of exercising one's curiosity and intelligence" rather than the love of wisdom.

- According to **Socrates**—"Philosophy is a daily activity."
- According to **Plato**—"Philosophy is the acquisition of knowledge."
- According to **Aristotle** "Philosophy is a science which discovers the real nature of supernatural elements."
- According to **Michael S. Russo**—Philosophy is a critical examination of reality characterized by rational inquiry that aims at the Truth for the sake of attaining wisdom."
- According to **Karl Marks**—"Philosophy is the interpretation of the world in order to change it."
- According to **Herbert Spencer**—"Philosophy is concerned with everything as a universal science."

- According to **John Dewey**—"Philosophy is not a panacea (remedy for all kinds of diseases/troubles) for the problems of men, but is that which emerges out of the methods employed by them to solve their problems."
- According to **Henderson**—"Philosophy is a rigorous, disciplined, guarded analysis of some of the most difficult problems which men have ever faced."
- According to **Anthony Kenny**—"Philosophy is thinking as clearly as possible about the most fundamental concepts that reach through all the disciplines."
- According to **Dr. Radhakrishnan**—"Philosophy is a view of life. It gives a direction to life, offers a design for living."
- **Milton K. Munitz** suggests that "philosophy is a quest for a view of the world and of man's place in it, which is arrived at and supported in a critical and logical way."
- According to **Bramold**—"Philosophy is a persistent effort of both ordinary and persistent people to make life as intelligible and meaningful as possible."
- According to **Don Cupitt**—"Philosophy is critical thinking: trying to become aware of how one's own thinking works, of all the things one takes for granted, of the way in which one's own thinking shapes the things one's thinking about."

1.5 Branches of Philosophy

According to Dr. Barry F. Vaughan, the major sub-disciplines of Philosophy are:

1. Metaphysics (Beyond Physics: dealing with realities beyond the physical)
2. Epistemology (Theory of knowledge)
3. Logic (deals with reasoning)
4. Axiology (Philosophical study of value)

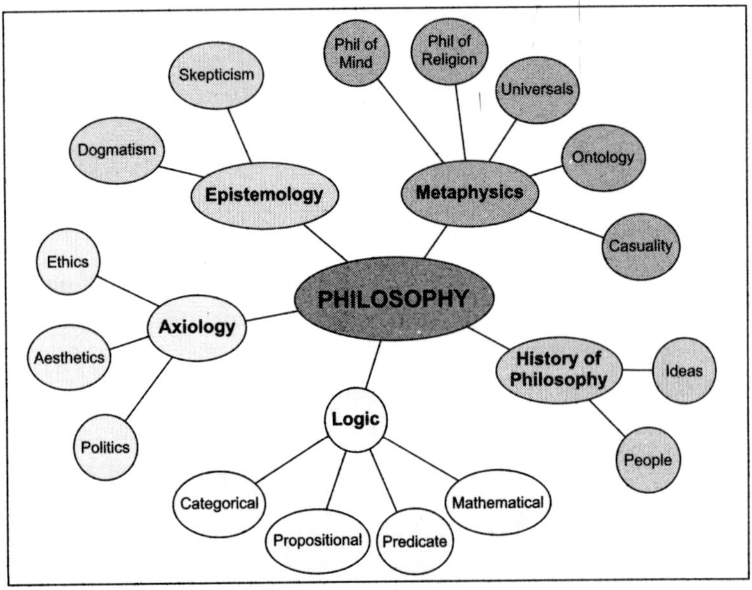

Picture Courtesy: Dr. Barry F. Vaughan.

Apart from these also a sub-branch of Philosophy is the History of this field which helped us to look into the journey of development of ideas.

5. *History of Philosophy* is the *philosophical* examination of the development of ***ideas*** it includes people and ideas.

People–What did philosophers of the past think about and why?

Ideas–How do ideas arise over time and influence the development of new ideas in the future?

1.5.1 Metaphysics

Metaphysics is the philosophical study of reality. The term is synonymous with "meta-empirical reality" that means the reality beyond the physical world. It is concerned with terrestrial and extra-terrestrial reality and the notion of "Being".

Metaphysics asks questions about the Nature of God, Spirits or even the Nature of Man.

The questions include—

> Does the soul exist?
>
> Where is the soul located in the human body?
>
> Is the soul synonymous with the mind?

Sub-branches of Metaphysics

Generally there are two sub-branches of Metaphysics:

a. General Metaphysics

b. Special Metaphysics

a. General Metaphysics: concerned with ontology

a.1. Ontology

"ontos"–Greek word for being.

It is concerned with the ontological nature of man.

This subject asks the question, *what kinds of things actually exist?*

b. Special Metaphysics

It includes the following:

b.1. Rational Psychology

It deals with philosophy of the human person.

It is concerned with things like the nature of dreams, memory and common sense as an inner sense?

Rational psychology deals with Philosophy of Mind which asks the question, *what is the nature of consciousness?*

b.2. Natural Theology (Theodicy)

"*Theos*"–Greek word for God

It is an attempt to study the Philosophy of Religion which asks the question, *What is the nature of God?*

b.3. Cosmology

"*Cosmos*"–Greek word for universe.

It is concerned with the study of the physical universe, its nature and origin.

This field gave birth to the philosophy of science.

1.5.2 Epistemology

Etymologically, "*episteme*"–Greek word for knowledge.

This sub-branch of philosophy is concerned with the study of knowledge.

It looks at the structure, source, the scope or limit knowledge.

This subject asks the questions like:

What is knowledge?
Can we have knowledge?
How do we get knowledge?

1.5.3 Axiology

This sub-branch of philosophy deals with the philosophical study of value:

Axiology is derived from the Greek word *axiă*, which means "value or worth" and *logia* is the philosophical study of value. The term was first used in the early 20th century by Paul Lapie, in 1902, and E. Von Hartmann, in 1908.

Lotze explained axiology as, "The general theory of value; the study of objects of interest".

John Warfield defines Axiology as, "The study of the nature of types and criteria of values and value judgment, especially in ethics".

In this way, we can say that Axiology is a branch of Philosophy dealing with:

Ethics, Aesthetics and ***Politics.***

a. Ethics investigates the concepts of right and good in individual and social conduct, i.e. the study of values in human conduct. It is concerned with how we ought to act.

This is the conduct of human person in the society. It deals with distinguishing between good and bad; moral and immoral.

Ethics is the philosophical study of morality. It asks the questions like:

> *What makes an action Right or Wrong?*
> *Is morality relative?*
> *What do the words 'right' and 'wrong' actually mean?*

b. Aesthetics is the study of values in art, i.e. it studies the concepts of beauty and harmony. Aesthetics is the philosophical study of beauty. It also includes the following:

- Philosophy of Literature
- Philosophy of Art
- Philosophy of Music

c. Politics is the study of "who gets what, when and how."

"Politika" is the Greek word which means affairs of the cities and it is the root of politics.

It comprises all the activities of co-operation, negotiation and conflicts within and between societies.

Political Theory is the philosophical study of justice.

1.5.4 Logic

It is derived from the greek word "*logike*" which means argumentative. Logic is the systematic study of forms of inference, the relations that lead to the acceptance of one proposition, the conclusion on the basis of a set of other propositions. It is the philosophical study of reason and arguments. It asks the questions like:

- What is an argument?
- What makes an argument work?
- What makes an argument fail?

1.6 Nature and Scope of Philosophy

As the philosophy is related to wisdom, it has already implied that the scope of philosophy cannot be put within precise boundary, but within the widening horizon of wisdom. Thus, the scope of philosophy embraces the whole of reality. Although philosophy claims to consider everything in general and nothing in particular, we can still point out some of the areas that are generally accepted as typically philosophical. By taking a quick glance at them, we will have clarified the scope of philosophy.

Metaphysics is the inquiry into the 'beyond' of physics, that seeks to ask and answer the most ultimate and fundamental questions about the whole of reality, the Divine, the human, and the cosmos. Metaphysical questions embrace everything as a whole. Thus, metaphysics occupies the foundational realm in philosophy.

Metaphysics questions the foundational truths of existence, such as the origin of the universe, evidence for supernatural phenomena, and whether God exists. Cultures have gone to war over disagreements about what they take to be religious truths; some people spend a lot of money to have psychic readings done, or communicate with dead relatives.

Another set of problems that philosophy has to consider are those connected with our thinking. There is, first of all, the study of valid thinking or argument, which is called 'logic'.

Epistemology is the study, not so much on what we know or how we know, but what it is to know. The study of good and evil too is a baffling question for the philosophers. It is the realm of morality. It does not enumerate the good and bad actions, but it makes a fundamental analysis as to what it is to be right or wrong. It enables the human mind to distinguish between what is good and what is bad; thus it is a fundamental search.

Epistemology grounds the sciences, concerned with issues like whether our perceptions are reliable, whether other people have minds like ours, what constitutes acceptable evidence, and whether past patterns of data provide sufficient support for future predictions.

Although cosmos is subjected to a thorough analysis in the wake of the growth of science, philosophy has not left it only to science. Complementing the scientific knowledge of the cosmos, philosophy too looks at it in its radicalism. Even though what has been traditionally developed as cosmology by Aristotle is differently looked at in today's scientific period, it continues to be a philosophical discipline. Reality includes not only cosmos, but the realms of the human and of the Divine as well.

Moral Theory reflects on what we value as right/wrong, or good/bad, and asks whether morality can exist without God, if all morality is relative to culture, and whether we see moral issues through a social lens of bias. Controversies such as female genital mutilation or whether assisted suicide is permissible demonstrate how complex moral thinking is once we think our way through different perspectives on the same problem.

Applied Ethics investigates how to use moral thinking in real-world situations. Should we separate conjoined twins knowing that one will die, when failure to separate means both will die? Should we eat meat? Should we use technology to design better babies? Very recently, for example, the gene manipulation mechanism known as CRISPR has made it possible to correct defects such as the inherited blood disorder beta-thalassemia in human embryos. This has ethicists sitting up and taking notice: should such "corrected" embryos be implanted in the womb? What happens to human society when only the rich can afford to manipulate embryos before implanting? Worse still, what if CRISPR is used commercially to create embryos with things like higher intelligence, better athleticism, and artistic ability? How we identify moral values and regulate institutional – and individual—practices in relation to them are very urgent and ongoing challenges for humanity.

1.7 Importance of Philosophy

Every human being has a philosophy of life; it gives shape to his/her life. Even those who do not find any importance for philosophy and question its relevance are in fact shouting aloud its importance by their use of it.

Raymont said, "Philosophy is an unceasing effort to discover the general truth that lies behind the particular fact, to discover also the realities that lie behind appearance."

Study of philosophy is not only for intellectual consumption, out of intellectual curiosity to know how others have philosophized, but also it is primarily for oneself to develop a philosophy of life. According to Richard Bradley, "Philosophy is 99 per cent about critical reflection on anything you care to be interested in."

Since one's philosophy of life moulds one's attitudes and convictions, it has to be developed, which is possible only by coming into contact with way in which philosophers have thought. As one gradually enters into the width of philosophy, one will experience its depth and importance as well. Just as philosophy cannot be confined within precise boundary.

The greatest advantage of philosophy consists in its ability to make the human mind sharp and disciplined. What one learns in philosophy may not be found as useful as other pieces of information from scientific and social fields. But what it does to human mind cannot be compared to the study of any other science. Study of philosophy gives a depth in one's thinking and acting in life.

Besides giving depth, philosophy disciplines the mind in such a way that it is able to understand every other discipline of knowledge.

Philosophy enables a person to have the clarity of concepts and precision of expressions. Such a precision and clarity will be seen in thinking, speaking and acting. Thus, philosophy enters the practical life as well.

1.8 Moral Philosophy

Morals are the welfare principles enunciated by the wise people, based on their experience and wisdom. They were edited, changed or modified or evolved to suit the geography of the region, rulers (dynasty), and in accordance with development of knowledge in science and technology and with time.

Morality is concerned with principles and practices of morals, such as:

(a) What ought or ought not to be done in a given situation?

(b) What is right or wrong about the handling of a situation?

(c) What is good or bad about the people, policies, and ideals involved?

- Morals are the principles on which one's judgments of right and wrong are based.
- These principles are derivable from full-fledged religious, cultural or political systems of belief.
- Morality is more fluid, personal and subjective.
- Morals are the social, cultural and religious beliefs or values of an individual or group which tells us what is right or wrong.
- They are the rules and standards made by the society or culture which is to be followed by us while deciding what is right.

Some Examples of Morals

- *Do not cheat*
- *Be loyal*
- *Be patient*
- *Always tell the truth*
- *Be generous*

Generally, morals refer to the beliefs what is not objectively right, but what is considered right for any situation, so it can be said that what is morally correct may not be objectively correct. Morals are not the hard and fast rules or very rigid, but they are the rules which a majority of people considered as right.

1.9 Ethics

Any society when it develops, it has to observe certain codes of conduct. Otherwise a society cannot progress. If everybody kills everybody else, there will be no peaceful society. If everybody steals there will be no normal growth of economy. So we need certain codes of conduct, which will control the people. It means moral codes of conduct.

Now-a-days, everywhere the term ethics is widely used. All persons whether in business, government, university or any other enterprise are concerned with ethics.

Different "definitions" of ethics are in use daily by the general public. Here, right or wrong, are a few to ponder:

(a) Ethics is adherence to the spirit and the letter of the law. People who claim that they "have done nothing wrong" after they are caught in a legal but unsavoury action often use this interpretation of ethics.
(b) Ethics is adherence to a religious belief.
(c) Ethics is adherence to "community or cultural standards."
(d) Ethics is adherence to my ideas.

> **Ethics** is a branch of philosophy dealing with values relating to human conduct with respect to the rightness or wrongness of certain actions.

1.10 Concept of Ethics

- By the term 'ethics' we mean a branch of moral philosophy– a sense of rightness or wrongness of actions, motives and the results of these actions.
- Ethics is a philosophical concept. Generally, 'ethics' and 'morals' have been used for same meaning in literature.
- The reason is behind that both the concepts have been derived etymologically from Latin and Greek words with similar meaning (Rohr, 1978).

- These concepts are interrelated and cannot be understood in isolation of one another (Khan, 1995).
- In fact, it deals with moral duty and obligation (Levine, 1990).

- In Webster's Ninth New Collegiate Dictionary ethics is defined as "the discipline dealing with what is good and bad and with moral duty and obligation."
- According to Bowman, "...ethics is action, the way we practice our values, a guidance system to be used in making decisions."
- Ethics is work—the labour of the individual and organizations trying to live up to closely held beliefs..." (Bowman, 1991).
- On the other hand, Dollery (1997) states that "ethics is not mysterious (but is) a part of everyday life."
- It is more apparent in the statement of Singer. He remarks, "Ethics, though not consciously created, is a product of social life, which has a function of promoting values common to the members of society."
- Ethical judgments "do this praising and encouraging action within these values" (Singer, 1990).

In contrast, ethicists use definitions that are more complex and may contain elements of all these common notions about what is ethical and what is not. It is not practical here to make a blanket definition of ethics because many have devoted their professional lives to that goal. Each of the authors in this series will make their own views clear on that subject.

The system addresses the questions of the human morality, such as: What should be a standard way for people to live? Or what are the appropriate actions in the given situations? What should be an ideal human conduct? etc.

- Ethics are widely accepted principles of right conduct.
- Ethics are more practical, conceived as overarching principles promoting fairness and forming the basis of criminal jurisprudence.

- Ethics are values which are based on greater objectivity and are geared towards ensuring smooth day-to-day functioning.
- Ethics is a branch of philosophy that deals with the principles of conduct of an individual or group. It works as a guiding principle as to decide what is good or bad.
- Ethics are the standards which govern the life of a person.
- Ethics is also known as moral philosophy.

1.11 Branches of Ethics

Under Ethics there are four important subject areas of study:

- **Meta-ethics:** Ethical philosophy that analyses the meaning and scope of moral values.
- **Descriptive Ethics:** The branch of ethics that deals with psychology, sociology, anthropology, etc.
- **Normative Ethics:** The study of the moral course of action through practical means.
- **Applied Ethics:** This branch tells us how we can achieve moral outcomes, in a particular circumstance.

1.12 Some Examples of Ethics

- *Truthfulness*
- *Honesty*
- *Loyalty*
- *Respect*
- *Fairness*
- *Integrity*

Every single individual has some principles which help him throughout his life to cope up with any adverse situation; they are known as ethics.

Ethics and Values together lay the foundation for sustainability. While they are sometimes used synonymously, they are different, wherein **ethics** are the set of rules that govern the behaviour of a person, established by a group or culture. **Values** refer to the beliefs for which a person has an enduring preference. Ethics and values are important in every aspect of life, when we have to make a choice between two things, wherein ethics determine what is right, values determine what is important.

In the world of intense competition, every business entity works on certain principles and beliefs which are nothing but the values. Likewise, ethics is implemented in the organization to ensure the protection of the interest of stakeholders like customers, suppliers, employees, society and government.

1.13 Aspects of Ethics

Generally ethics are of two types:

(i) Personal Ethics, and

(ii) Business Ethics.

1.13.1 Personal Ethics

Personal ethics has been referred as the rules by which an individual lives his or her personal life.

1.13.2 Business Ethics

Business ethics is concerned with truth and justice and has a variety of aspects such as the expectations of society and competition, advertising, public relations, social responsibilities, consumer autonomy and corporate behaviour in the home country as well as abroad (Weihrich and Koontz, 1994).

1.14 Applied Aspects of Ethics

The following are two of the most important applied aspects of ethics:

(i) Professional Ethics, and

(ii) Administrative Ethics.

1.14.1 Professional Ethics

- Professional ethics are a set of norms that determine an individual position towards professional duties, professional relations with other employees and finally, towards society as a whole.
- It reflects the specifics of morality, personal interrelations and behaviour coming from professional activities.

It is the existence of special personal relations within professional groups that results in special moral norms regulating these relations. It includes behavioural codes defining certain types of moral relations between individuals who consider these codes optimal for the performance of a professional duty and the ground for these codes is the social and psychological interpretation of cultural and humanistic purposes of the profession.

1.14.2 Administrative Ethics

One of the most important areas of applied ethics is 'administrative ethics' which implies general moral rules to specific sphere of human relations.

- It involves the application of moral principles to the conduct of officials in organizations.
- Normally, it stresses the governmental employees set up ethical standards for managerial decisions, analyze these standards and bear personal and professional responsibility for the decisions made.
- More specifically, administrative ethics assume that individuals in organizations can make moral judgments and can be the objects of moral judgments.

Two common views of administration—that administrators should either follow the policies of an organization or resign from office, and that administrators should not be held morally responsible for the wrongs of their organizations—deny these assumptions and would make administrative ethics impossible. By understanding how these views themselves are mistaken, we can see how administrative ethics is possible and what forms it should take (Thompson, 1985). Administrative ethics studies all aspects of employees of public administration and the activities of all the senior managers in all organizations. It bears the following three basic components.

Table 1.1: Basic Components of Administrative Ethics

Components	*Explanation*
Values	Individual, group and social statements, opinion and attitudes towards concepts like freedom, justice, honesty, loyalty, and responsibility.
Standards and Norms	The principles that guideline the action of the people and employees and help lead and control their behaviour.
Behaviour	Different forms of activity limited by certain standards and norms corresponding with social values.

2

Professional Ethics and Scientific Conduct

"Ethics is knowing the difference between what you have right to do and what is right to do." — *Potter Stewart*

2.0 Professional Ethics

Profession is a commitment to a designated and organized occupation by virtue of being an authority over a body of knowledge with requisite skills acquired through specialized training.

An occupation becomes a profession when a group of people sharing the same occupation work together in a morally acceptable way with members setting and following a certain ethics code. A professional is a practitioner belonging to a specific profession.

- Professional ethics, as opposed to personal values and morality, is a set of ethical standards and values a practicing engineer is required to follow.
- It sets the standards for professional practice, and is only learned in a professional school or while practicing one's own profession.

Today, it is an essential part of professional education because it helps students deal with issues they will face.

2.1 Concept and Meaning

The word 'prophes' is derived from the Greek word "*prophaino*" which means to declare public. This Greek word prophaino became the Latin word "*prophesions*"—a word that was used to refer to public statements made by persons who sought to occupy positions of public class.

A profession, however, can be defined generally as: "a vocation/occupation requiring advanced knowledge in a particular field and whose practice meets the highest standards of the profession."

A professional, therefore, is an individual with a high level of skill or knowledge in a particular field and whose practice meets the highest standards of the profession.

Profession was meant to bind the person uttering it but not the listening to act to help those seeking particular types of assistance. Individuals, therefore, become professionals by virtue of what they profess or publicly proclaim before other people who claim a particular knowledge or skill that the professionals have.

Lowenberg defines **professional ethics** as a qualification of the special obligations that arise out of a person's voluntary choice to become a professional. It, therefore, identifies and describes the ethical behaviours expected of professional practitioners.

2.2 Objectives of Professional Ethics

The prime objective is to increase one's ability to deal effectively with moral complexity in managerial practice. It is intended to develop a set of beliefs, attitudes, and habits that engineers should display concerning morality.

Professional Ethics helps us—	
1.	To understand the moral values that ought to guide the profession,
2.	To resolve the moral issues in the profession, and
3.	To justify the moral judgment concerning the profession.
4.	To provide guidance in the practice of the profession especially where the practitioners are faced with practice dilemmas.
5.	To protect members of the public from charlatans and quacks.
6.	To promote harmony and brotherhood within the profession.
7.	To help professionals avoid litigations, i.e. to its members who are sued for malpractice.
8.	To protect the profession from external control, especially government control, because many professionals have realized that self-control is more important than governmental control.

Alternatively, the objectives of the study on Professional Ethics may be listed as:

(A) Improvement of the Cognitive Skills (Skills of the Intellect in Thinking Clearly)

1. Moral awareness (proficiency in recognizing moral problems).
2. Cogent moral reasoning (comprehending, assessing different views).
3. Moral coherence (forming consistent viewpoints based on facts).

4. Moral imagination (searching beyond obvious the alternative responses to issues and being receptive to creative solutions).
5. Moral communication, to express and support one's views to others.

(B) To Act in Morally Desirable Ways, Towards Moral Commitment and Responsible Conduct

6. Moral reasonableness, i.e. willing and able to be morally responsible.
7. Respect for persons, which means showing concern for the well-being of others, besides oneself.
8. Tolerance of diversity, i.e. respect for ethnic and religious differences, and acceptance of reasonable differences in moral perspectives.
9. Moral hope, i.e. believes in using rational dialogue for resolving moral conflicts.
10. Integrity, which means moral integrity, and integrating one's professional life and personal convictions.

2.3 Professional Values

Lowenberg argues that professional values need to be derivable and in conformity with the general societal values, although he acknowledges that in some cases, however, there might be some differences in emphasis, practices and interpretation.

Among the core values for professionals are the following:

1. Regard for individual integrity.
2. Respect for individual rights and autonomy.
3. Commitment to making social institutions more humane and responsive to human needs.
4. Respect for and acceptance of unique characteristics of diverse populations.
5. Responsibility for one's own ethical conduct and nobility for practice.

2.4 Ethical Values in Professionalism

A profession is one which by virtue of the fact that its members adhere to a distinct ethical guidance in the course of their practice. Therefore, every profession must have certain core values at the centre of its practice.

According to Colin Albert, the core values of Profession are the following:

1. Trustworthiness

Professionals are thought to be trustworthy by the public either because they are experts or because they are service providers to public good.

They require a number of values or virtues, e.g. honesty, integrity, loyalty and reliability.

(a) Honesty

It requires a commitment to convey the truth as you know it best and avoid any communication that can mislead or deceive.

There are two dimensions of honesty:

- (i) Truthfulness—the intention not to misrepresent a fact.
- (ii) clear commitments—be sure that when you are making a commitment the person understands.

(b) Loyalty

It is the responsibility to promote the interests of your profession or affiliation, i.e. by safeguarding confidential information and avoid conflict.

2. Respect

Every person has a right to be treated with dignity. Respect is about honouring the essential world of all people including oneself. We are morally obligated to treat everyone with respect regardless of who they are or what they have done. Respect requires civility, courtesy, tolerance and decency when dealing with humanity.

3. Responsibility

Responsibility is the relation between the act and the agent as doer of the act, as answerable or accountable for that act. The degree of agent's control over his/her act can be lessened by what are called modifiers of responsibility.

These are:

(a) Ignorance affecting the knowledge.
(b) Strong emotions affecting the consent of the will.
(c) Intellectual fear opposing the will, a contrary wish.

Responsibility requires the following:

i. Accountability
ii. Pursuit of excellence
iii. Perseverance
iv. Continuous improvement
v. Self-restraint

4. Fairness

This is the form of justice where due considerations should be given to all without any bias or discrimination.

The following are required:

(a) *Process*—Using open/unbiased processes when evaluating problems.
(b) *Impartiality*—Decisions should be unbiased without favouritism and prejudice.
(c) *Equity*—Not taking advantage over weakness or ignorance of others.

5. Decency

Professionals must ensure that their profession is always decent and they do not allow indecency. In order for humans to live as human beings, they ought to observe a certain minimum ethical requirement below which their human right is violated.

6. Accuracy

Professionals must practice their profession with tooth-comb accuracy. Accuracy has to do with getting issue rightly, i.e. by figures, facts, names, claims etc. Always meticulous attention must be paid to details and be careful even about small things like spelling of names, figures, sequences of event.

7. Kindness

Kindness can also be generally seen as one's concern with the good of others and not necessarily their own. It has an element of concern for others and a willingness to assist those who are disadvantaged.

2.5 Integrity

- Integrity is defined as the unity of thought, word and deed (honesty) and open-mindedness.
- It includes the capacity to communicate the factual information so that others can make well-informed decisions.
- It yields the person's 'peace of mind', and hence adds strength and consistency in character, decisions, and actions. This paves way to one's success.

It is one of the self-direction virtues. It enthuses people not only to execute a job well but to achieve excellence in performance. It helps them to own the responsibility and earn self-respect and recognition by doing the job. Moral integrity is defined as a virtue, which reflects a consistency of one's attitudes, emotions, and conduct in relation to justified moral values.

Integrity comes in many forms, but honesty and dependability are two traits that are expected in most workplace situations. Without responsible behaviour, distrust can make a work environment tense and uncomfortable. A strong work ethic shows co-workers and clients that you are reliable and take your responsibilities seriously. Polite communication, respectable behaviour and fiscal responsibility also help you stand out as a trustworthy employee.

2.5.1 Research Integrity

The Singapore Statement on Research Integrity, written during the Second World Congress on Research Integrity, presents "principles and professional responsibilities that are fundamental to the integrity of research wherever it is undertaken."

Three sets of obligations of researchers to adhere to professional standards:

1. An obligation to honour the trust that their colleagues place in them.
2. An obligation to themselves. Irresponsible conduct in research can make it impossible to achieve a goal.
3. An obligation to act in ways that serve the public.

2.6 Intellectual Honesty

We have a moral duty to be honest. This duty is especially important when we share ideas that can inform or persuade others. Intellectual honesty is honesty in the acquisition, analysis, and transmission of ideas. A person is being intellectually honest when he or she, knowing the truth, states that truth.

Intellectual honesty pertains to any communication intended to inform or persuade. This includes all forms of scholarship, consequential conversations such as dialogue, debate, negotiations, product and service descriptions, various forms of persuasion, and public communications such as announcements, speeches, lectures, instruction, presentations, publications, declarations, briefings, news releases, policy statements, reports, religious instructions, social media posts, and journalism including not only prose and speech, but graphs, photographs, and other means of expression.

Intellectual Honesty combines good faith with a primary motivation towards seeking true beliefs.

Harvard ethicist Louis M. Guenin describes the "kernel" of intellectual honesty to be "a virtuous disposition to eschew deception when given an incentive for deception."

Intellectual honesty is an applied method of problem solving, characterized by an unbiased, honest attitude, which can be demonstrated in a number of different ways including:

- Ensuring support for chosen ideologies does not interfere with the pursuit of truth;
- Relevant facts and information are not purposefully omitted even when such things may contradict one's hypothesis;
- Facts are presented in an unbiased manner, and not twisted to give misleading impressions or to support one view over another; and
- References, or earlier work, are acknowledged where possible, and plagiarism is avoided.

The fundamentals of having intellectual honesty are as follows:

- Exercise moral virtue,
- find the facts, increase respect,
- seek insights, and
- search for common ground whenever you share ideas with others.

2.7 Intellectual Dishonesty

Dishonesty is the alternative to intellectual honesty. Learn to identify dishonesty and challenge it in yourself and others. Common forms of intellectual dishonesty include:

Intentionally committed fallacies and deception in debates and reasoning are called intellectual dishonesty.

Because false beliefs are often harmful, we have moral obligation to seek true beliefs. Challenge dishonesty in yourself and others.

1. **Plagiarism**—The wrongful appropriation of others language, thought, ideas, or expressions.
2. **Selective reporting**—Selecting and reporting only the information that supports a single point of view or conclusion. This includes publication bias, media bias, and various forms of censorship.
3. **Disinformation**—Spreading false information with the intent to deceive.
4. **Fabrication, including falsifying data**—Incorrectly reporting results or selectively omitting data in an attempt to prove a hypothesis or to support a position.
5. **Logical fallacies**—Errors in reasoning often go unrecognized and unchallenged.
6. **Applying double standards**—Using different sets of principles for similar situations.
7. **Using false analogies**—Making unsound comparisons.
8. **Exaggeration and overgeneralization**—Stating an inductive generalization based on insufficient evidence.
9. **Presenting straw man arguments**—Giving the impression of refuting an opponent's argument, while actually refuting an argument that was not presented by that opponent.
10. **Poisoning the well**—Sharing irrelevant or untrue adverse information about the presenter.
11. **Quoting out of context**—Removing a passage from its surrounding matter in such a way as to distort its intended meaning.

12. **Bias**—Silently omitting, suppressing, excluding, or discounting evidence or viewpoints contrary to the argument you are making or the ideology you are defending. Bias is a failure to remain objective and maintain a neutral point of view.
13. **Statistical bias**—Drawing conclusions from an unrepresentative sample.
14. **Cherry picking**—pointing to individual cases or data that appear to confirm a particular position while ignoring a significant portion of related cases or data that may contradict that position.
15. **Half-truths**—Making a deceptive statement that includes some element of truth.
16. **Data dredging**—Presenting patterns uncovered in data as being statistically significant without first devising a specific hypothesis as to the underlying causality.

2.8 Professional Codes of Ethics

A code of ethics prescribes how professionals are to pursue their common ideal so that each may do the best at a minimal cost to oneself and those they care about.

The code is to protect each professional from certain pressures (for example, the pressure to cut corners to save money) by making it reasonably likely (and more likely than otherwise) that most other members of the profession will not take advantage. A code is a solution to a coordination problem. A professional has obligations to the employer, to customers, to other professionals—colleagues with specific expectations of reciprocity.

2.9 Scientific Conduct

Conduct means a mode or standard of personal behaviour especially as based on moral principles or the act, manner, or process of carrying on certain responsibilities. When it is applied in the fields of scientific work we call it as scientific conduct.

Scientific conduct is defined by three overarching principles—

- Honesty
- Transparency
- Accountability

2.10 Principles for Good Scientific Practice

All researches carried out in the globe must be of high quality and reliability. A part of conducting reliable research of high quality is in compliance with the principles for good scientific practice. These principles are understood partly through a description of unwanted behaviour, defined as either scientific misconduct or questionable research practice, and partly through guidelines for what behaviours are wanted in connection with, e.g. publishing research results and attribution of authorship.

So we can understand that the Scientific conduct, Research Ethics and publication ethics are so closely related. But we will discuss them separately in order to make a clear concept on those topics.

2.11 Scientific Misconduct

Behaviour that would be considered scientific misconduct could occur at all points in a research protocol. You could encounter different types of scientific misconduct at different stages, right from the origination of the research study itself to the publication of the results.

Scientific misconduct is a deliberate or grossly negligent breach of the standards for scientific conduct in scientific research. It is the violation of the standard codes of scholarly conduct and ethical behaviour in the publication of professional scientific research.

Danish definition:

"Scientific misconduct is the intention or gross negligence leading to fabrication of the scientific message or a false credit or emphasis given to a scientist."

Swedish definition:

"Scientific misconduct is the intentional distortion of the research process by fabrication of data, text, hypothesis, or methods from another researcher's manuscript form or publication; or distortion of the research process in other ways."

The law on scientific misconduct defines this through mainly three types of unacceptable behaviour:

Fabrication: Unreported construction of data or substitution for fictitious data.

Falsification: Manipulation of research material, equipment or processes, as well as changing or leaving out data or results, whereby the research appears misleading.

Plagiarism: Acquisition of other people's ideas, processes, results, texts or special terms without appropriate accreditation.

2.12 Causes of Scientific Misconducts

According to David Goodstein of Caltech, there are motivators for scientists to commit misconduct, which are briefly summarised here.

Career Pressure

Science is still a very strongly career-driven discipline. Scientists depend on a good reputation to receive ongoing support and funding, and a good reputation relies largely on the publication of high-profile scientific papers. Hence, there is a strong imperative to "publish or perish". Clearly, this may motivate desperate (or fame-hungry) scientists to fabricate results.

Ease of Fabrication

In many scientific fields, results are often difficult to reproduce accurately, being obscured by noise, artifacts, and other extraneous data. That means that even if a scientist does falsify data, they can expect to get away with it—or at least claim innocence if their results conflict with others in the same field. There are no "scientific police" who are trained to fight scientific crimes; all investigations are made by experts in science but amateurs in dealing with criminals. It is relatively easy to cheat although difficult to know exactly how many scientists fabricate data.

2.13 Danish Committee for Scientific Misconduct

It covers six main aspects of good scientific practice:

1. Research planning and conduct
2. Data management
3. Publication and communication
4. Authorship
5. Collaborative research
6. Conflicts of interest

Failure to comply with the principles for good scientific practice may constitute questionable research practice or scientific misconduct.

In Denmark, cases involving scientific misconduct are handled by the Danish Committee for Scientific Misconduct. The Committee only handles cases, which are significant for Danish research, meaning cases involving research conducted at a Danish institution, by Danish scientists or research financed by Danish funding bodies.

A case can be raised by submission of a formal complaint, or you can request that the Committee takes up a case, in order for you to be cleared of charges in the form of circulating rumours. Each year the Committee produces an annual review of their decisions.

2.14 Common Types of Scientific Misconduct

Listed below are the top 10 transgressions that peer reviewers and journal editors look for, incorporating content from both the World Association of Medical Editors (WAME), and the US Office of Research Integrity (ORI):

1. **Misappropriation of Ideas**—Taking the intellectual property of others, perhaps as a result of reviewing someone else's article or manuscript, or grant application and proceeding with the idea as your own.
2. **Plagiarism**—Utilizing someone else's words, published work, research processes, or results without giving appropriate credit *via* full citation.
3. **Self-plagiarism**—Recycling or re-using your own work without appropriate disclosure and/or citation.
4. **Impropriety of Authorship**—Claiming undeserved authorship on your own behalf, excluding material contributors from co-authorship, including non-contributors as authors, or submitting multi-author papers to journals without the consensus of all named authors.
5. **Failure to Comply with Legislative and Regulatory Requirements**—Wilful violations of rules concerning the safe use of chemicals, care of human and animal test subjects, inappropriate use of investigative drugs or equipment, and inappropriate use of research funds.
6. **Violation of Generally Accepted Research Practices**—This can include the proposal of the research study, manipulation of experiments to generate preferred results, deceptive statistical or analytical practices to generate preferred results, or improper reporting of results to present a misleading outcome.
7. **Falsification of Data**—Rather than manipulate the experiments or the data to generate preferred results, this transgression simply fabricates the data entirely.

8. **Failure to Support Validation of Your Research**—By refusing to supply complete datasets or research material needed to facilitate validation of your results through a replication study.
9. **Failure to Respond to Known Cases of Unsuccessful Validation Attempts**—Published research that is found to be flawed should be retracted from the journal that published it.
10. **Inappropriate Behaviour in Relation to Suspected Misconduct**—Failure to cooperate with any claims of misconduct made against you, failure to report known or suspected misconduct, destruction of any evidence related to any claim of misconduct, retaliation against any person involved in a claim of misconduct, knowingly making false claims of misconduct.

2.15 Procedure of Scientific Research

If we see the process involved in scientific research process at a glance, the following issues are involved there:

Part I. Sharing Scientific Knowledge

- Research Publication
- Authorship and Collaborative Research
- Scientific Misconduct—FFP & QRP

Part II. Laboratory Practice and COI

- Practices of Image and Data Manipulation
- Data Ownership and Intellectual Property Guidelines
- Conflict of Interest and Commitment
- Govt. *vs.* Industry Sponsored Research
- Sharing the Data in Thesis

Sharing Scientific Knowledge

The object of research is to extend human knowledge beyond what is already known. But an individual's knowledge enters the domain of science only after it is presented to others in such a fashion that they can independently judge its validity. (NAP, "On Being a Scientist" 1995)

"Science is a shared knowledge based on a common understanding of some aspect of the physical or social world."

Presentations

- Social conventions play an important role in establishing the reliability of scientific knowledge.

Publications in Peer Reviewed Journals

- Research results are privileged until they are published.

Thesis

(NAP, "On Being a Scientist" 1995)

Research Publication

"A paper is an organized description of hypotheses, data and conclusions, intended to instruct the reader. If your research does not generate papers, it might just as well not have been done" (G. Whitesides, Adv. Mater., 2004)

"If it wasn't published, it wasn't done"— in E.H. Miller, 1993

2.16 Scientific Misconduct—FFP & QRP

2.16.1 Falsification, Fabrication, and Plagiarism (FFP)

The U.S. National Science Foundation defines three types of research misconduct: fabrication, falsification, and plagiarism.

Fabrication is making up results and recording or reporting them. This is sometimes referred to as "dry labbing". A more minor form of fabrication is where references are included to give arguments the appearance of widespread acceptance, but are actually fake, or do not support the argument.

Falsification is manipulating research materials, equipment, or processes or changing or omitting data or results such that the research is not accurately represented in the research record.

Plagiarism is the appropriation of another person's ideas, processes, results, or words without giving appropriate credit. One form is the appropriation of the ideas and results of others, and publishing as to make it appear the author had performed all the work under which the data was obtained. A subset is citation plagiarism—wilful or negligent failure to appropriately credit other or prior discoverers, so as to give an improper impression of priority. This is also known as, "citation amnesia", the "disregard syndrome" and "bibliographic negligence".

Arguably, this is the most common type of scientific misconduct. Sometimes, it is difficult to guess whether authors intentionally ignored a highly relevant cite or lacked knowledge of the prior work. Discovery credit can also be inadvertently reassigned from the original discoverer to a better-known researcher. This is a special case of the Matthew effect.

Plagiarism-fabrication—The act of taking an unrelated figure from an unrelated publication and reproducing it exactly in a new publication, claiming that it represents new data.

Self-plagiarism—Or multiple publication of the same content with different titles or in different journals is sometimes also considered misconduct; scientific journals explicitly ask authors not to do this. It is referred to as "salami" (i.e. many identical slices) in the jargon of medical journal editors. According to some editors this includes publishing the same article in a different language.

2.16.2 Questionable Research Practice (QRP)

Questionable research practices are behaviours which may negatively influence the quality of the research conducted, or which at the very least may raise questions about its credibility. An important thing to understand about questionable research practices is that they may occur even if there is no intention to deceive, but simply as a result of carelessness.

Questionable research practice is defined in the law on scientific misconduct as "Any breach of commonly accepted standards for responsible conduct in research, including the standards described in the Danish Code of Conduct for Research integrity and other relevant institutional, national or international practices and guidelines for integrity in research."

Examples of questionable research practice are:

- Conscious or unconscious bias
- Sloppy research methods or analyses
- Ignoring ethical guidelines
- Denying attribution of authorship to qualifying contributors.

Thus, questionable research practice represents a grey area between ideal behaviour and scientific misconduct.

2.17 Practices of Image Manipulation

Compared to other forms of scientific misconduct, image fraud (manipulation of images to distort their meaning) is of particular interest since it can frequently be detected by external parties. Image manipulations are typically done on visually repetitive images such as those of western blots, histologies or data visualisations like graphs.

In general, the following photo manipulations are not allowed:

1. Splicing together different images to represent a single experiment.
2. Changing brightness and contrast of only a part of the image.
3. Any change that conceals information, even when it is considered to be aspecific, which includes:
   (i) changing brightness and contrast to leave only the most intense signal.
   (ii) using clone tools to hide information.
   (iii) showing only a very small part of the photograph so that additional information is not visible.

In 2006, the *Journal of Cell Biology* gained publicity for instituting tests to detect photo manipulation in papers that were being considered for publication. This was in response to the increased usage of programmes such as Adobe Photoshop by scientists, which facilitate photo manipulation.

2.18 Other Types of Research Misconduct are also recognized:

1. **Ghostwriting**—the phenomenon where someone other than the named author(s) makes a major contribution. Typically, this is done to mask contributions from authors with a conflict of interest.
2. Conversely, research misconduct is not limited to not listing authorship, but also includes the act of **conferring authorship** on those that have not made substantial contributions to the research. This is much harder to prove due to a lack of consistency in defining "authorship" or "substantial contribution".
3. Scientific misconduct can also occur during the peer-review process by a reviewer or editor with a conflict of interest.
4. Coercive citation can also inflate the perceived citation impact of a researcher's work and their reputation in the scientific community, similar to excessive self-citation. Reviewers are expected to be impartial and assess the quality of their work. They are expected to declare a conflict of interest to the editors if they are colleagues or competitors of the authors.

2.19 Responsibly to Avoid Scientific Misconduct

2.19.1 Responsibility of Authors and of Coauthors

All authors of a scientific publication are expected to have made reasonable attempts to check findings submitted to academic journals for publication.

Guest authorship (where there is stated authorship in the absence of involvement, also known as gift authorship) and ghost authorship (where the real author is not listed as an author) are commonly regarded as forms of research misconduct.

2.19.2 Responsibilities of Research Institutions

In general, defining whether an individual is guilty of misconduct requires a detailed investigation by the individual's employing academic institution. Such investigations require detailed and rigorous processes and can be extremely costly. Furthermore, the more senior the individual under suspicion, the more likely it is that conflicts of interest will compromise the investigation.

2.19.3 Responsibilities of Uninvolved Scientific Colleagues

Some academics believe that scientific colleagues who suspect scientific misconduct should consider taking informal action themselves, or reporting their concerns. This question is of great importance since much research suggests that it is very difficult for people to act or come forward when they see unacceptable behaviour, unless they have help from their organizations.

2.19.4 Responsibility of Journals

Journals are responsible for safeguarding the research record and hence have a critical role in dealing with suspected misconduct. This is recognised by the Committee on Publication Ethics (COPE) which has issued clear guidelines on the form (e.g. retraction) that concerns over the research record should take.

The COPE guidelines state that journal editors should consider retracting a publication if they have clear evidence that the findings are unreliable, either as a result of misconduct (e.g. data fabrication) or honest error (e.g. miscalculation or experimental error). Retraction is also appropriate in cases of redundant publication, plagiarism and unethical research.

2.20 Examples of Scientific Misconduct in Literature

1. **Bharat Aggarwal (US)**, a former Ransom Horne, Jr. Distinguished Professor of Cancer Research at the University of Texas MD Anderson Cancer Center, resigned his position after fraud was discovered in 65 papers published by him in the area of curcumin as a treatment for cancer. Aggarwal has had 28 of his publications retracted.
2. **Elias Alsabti (Iraq, US)** was a medical practitioner who posed as a biomedical researcher. He plagiarized as many as 60 papers in the field of cancer research, many with non-existent co-authors.
3. **Joachim Boldt (Germany)**, an anesthesiologist formerly based at the Justus Liebig University, Giessen, was stripped of his professorship and criminally investigated for forgery in his research studies. Boldt has had 96 of his publications retracted.
4. **John Darsee** (US), a cardiologist formerly based at Harvard University, fabricated data in published research articles and more than 100 abstracts and book chapters. In 1983, Darsee was disbarred for ten years by the US National Institute of Health. Darsee has had at least 17 of his publications retracted.
5. **Dipak Das** (US), former Director of the Cardiovascular Research Center at the University of Connecticut Health Center, was found in a University investigation to be guilty of 145 counts of fabrication or falsification of research data. Das has had 20 of his publications retracted.
6. **Evan B. Dreyer** (US), former Associate Professor of Ophthalmology at Harvard University Medical School, reported falsified and/or fabricated experimental results in manuscripts and grant applications. In 2000, Dreyer was blocked for 10 years from receiving NIH-sponsored research grants.

7. **Terry Elton (US)**, Professor of Pharmacology at Ohio State University, was found guilty of scientific misconduct by both a University Committee and the Office of Research Integrity. Elton has had seven of his publications retracted.
8. **Woo-suk Hwang (Hwang Woo-suk) (South Korea)**, former Professor of Biotechnology at Seoul National University, was found by a University Committee to have committed "deliberate fabrication" in his research on stem cells, and to have coerced female members of his research team to donate their eggs. In 2009, Hwang was found guilty by the Seoul Central District Court of embezzlement and bioethical violations in connection to his research programme.
9. **Santosh Katiyar (US, India)**, former Associate Professor at the University of Alabama, Birmingham and the Birmingham VA Medical Center who investigated the effects of "natural products" upon cancer, was in 2017 dismissed from his academic positions following an institutional investigation that found evidence of image manipulation in 20 of his research papers, all of which UAB has called to be retracted. Katiyar has had 12 of his research papers retracted, and three others have received an expression of concern.
10. **Robert Weinberg (USA)**, a professor of Biology at MIT, was found to be responsible in five incidents of scientific misconduct involving falsification or fabrication of data. As of 2020, Weinberg has had five research papers retracted.
11. **Weishui Y. Weiser (US)**, a former Assistant Professor of Medicine at Harvard Medical School, falsified data supported by two Public Health Service (PHS) grants. Weiser has had at least four publications retracted.
12. **Guido Zadel (Germany)**, published an article with the title "Enantioselective Reactions in a Static Magnetic Field" in 1994. His experiments had been manipulated, which led to the retraction of the respective paper and the final loss of his doctoral degree in 2004. The German version of the article is still accessible at Angew. Chem. in 2018 for $59 without any obvious retraction note.

13. **Dănuț Marcu (Romania)**, a mathematician and computer scientist, was banned from publishing in several journals due to plagiarism. He had submitted a manuscript for publication that was a word-for-word copy of a published paper written by another author.
14. **Jan Hendrik Schön (Germany, US)**, a researcher in the physics of semiconductors formerly employed by Bell Labs, forged results by using the same data sets for different and unrelated experiments. Schön has had 32 of his publications retracted.
15. **Olivier Voinnet (France)** was suspended in 2015 for two years from the CNRS (the French National Centre for Scientific Research) due to multiple cases of data manipulation. In 2016, EMBO recalled the Gold Medal awarded to Voinnet in 2009. As of 2020, Voinnet has had nine research publications retracted, five other papers have received an expression of concern, and 25 other papers have been corrected.
16. **Jens Förster (Netherlands, Germany)**, a social psychologist formerly of the University of Amsterdam and the Ruhr-Universität, Bochum, fabricated data reported in a number of published papers. An investigating committee in 2015 identified in Förster's work data that were "practically impossible" and displayed "strong evidence for low veracity." Förster has had four of his research publications retracted, and three others have received an expression of concern.
17. **Bruno Frey (Switzerland)**, an economist formerly at the University of Zurich, in 2010-11 committed multiple acts of self-plagiarism in articles about the Titanic disaster. Frey admitted to the self-plagiarism, terming the acts "grave mistake" and "deplorable".

18. **Karen M. Ruggiero (US),** former Assistant Professor of Psychology at Harvard University, fabricated NIH-sponsored research data on gender and discrimination. Ruggiero has had two research publications retracted.
19. **Diederik Stapel (Netherlands),** former Professor of Social Psychology at Tilburg University, fabricated data in dozens of studies on human behaviour, a deception described by the *New York Times* as "an audacious academic fraud". Stapel has had 58 of his publications retracted.
20. In 2016, the scientific publisher Springer Nature retracted 58 papers from seven journals, authored mostly by Iran-based researchers, because the papers showed evidence of authorship manipulation, peer-review manipulation, and/or plagiarism.
21. Ohio University in 2006 alleged more than three dozen cases of plagiarism in master's degree theses dating back 20 years in its mechanical engineering department.

Source: https://en.wikipedia.org/wiki/List_of_scientific_misconduct_incidents

3

Research and Publication Ethics

"It takes less time to do things right than to explain why you did it wrong."
—*Henry W. Longfellow*

3.0 Research Ethics

The word 'Ethics' means moral principles of right and wrong. When it is involved in the field of Research, the concerned discipline is called Research Ethics.

Definition

> "Research ethics" refers to a diverse set of values, norms and institutional regulations that help constitute and regulate scientific activity.

"Research ethics" is simply incorporating the ethical principles into research practice which includes all stages from inception of research through to completion and publication of results and beyond.

Research ethics involves the application of fundamental ethical principles to a variety of topics involving research, including scientific research. These include the design and implementation of research involving human experimentation, animal experimentation, various aspects of academic scandal, including scientific misconduct (such as fraud, fabrication of data and plagiarism), whistle blowing, regulation of research etc.

3.1 History of Research Ethics

Research ethics is most developed as a concept in medical research. The key agreement here is the 1964 Declaration of Helsinki. The Nuremberg Code is a former agreement, but with many still important notes. Research in the social sciences presents a different set of issues than those in medical research.

Chronology

- 1947—Nuremberg Code
- 1968—Helsinki Declaration
- 1979—Belmont Report
- 1993—CIOMS (Council for International Organizations of Medical Sciences)
- 2005—UNESCO

The academic research enterprise is built on a foundation of trust. Researchers trust that the results reported by others are sound. Society trusts that the results of research reflect an honest attempt by scientists and other researchers to describe the world accurately and without bias. But this trust will endure only if the scientific community devotes itself to exemplifying and transmitting the values associated with ethical research conduct.

There are many ethical issues to be taken into serious consideration for research. Sociologists need to be aware of having the responsibility to secure the actual permission and interests of all those involved in the study. They should not misuse any of the information discovered, and there should be a certain moral responsibility maintained towards the participants.

There is a duty to protect the rights of people in the study as well as their privacy and sensitivity. The confidentiality of those involved in the observation must be carried out, keeping their anonymity and privacy secure. All of these ethics must be honoured unless there are other overriding reasons to do so—for example, any illegal or terrorist activity.

Research ethics in a medical context is dominated by principalism. Medical research involving human experimentation is overseen by an ethics committee, in most countries working under legislation based on the Declaration of Helsinki and its later revisions.

Research ethics is different throughout different types of educational communities. Every community has its own set of morals. In Anthropology research ethics were formed to protect those who are being researched and to protect the researcher from topics or events that may be unsafe or may make either party feel uncomfortable. It is a widely observed guideline that anthropologists use especially when doing ethnographic fieldwork.

3.2 Objectives of Research Ethics

- To protect human participants.
- To ensure that research is conducted in a way that serves interests of individuals, groups and/or society as a whole.
- To examine specific research activities and projects for their ethical soundness, protection of confidentiality and the process of informed consent.

3.3 Ethical Principles in Research

1. **Voluntary Participation** (Informed consent—components, deception—procedures).
2. **Non-maleficence**—Do no harm (commission or omission) minimize harm.
3. **PAC**: Privacy, Anonymity and Confidentiality.
4. **Beneficence**—Promotion of wellbeing (maximize benefit).
5. **Autonomy**—Make own decisions.
6. **Integrity**—Consistency of thought and action.

3.4 Codes and Policies for Research Ethics

There are different professional associations, government agencies, and universities which have adopted specific codes, rules, and policies relating to research ethics. Many government agencies, such as the National Institutes of Health (NIH), the National Science Foundation (NSF), the Food and Drug Administration (FDA), the Environmental Protection Agency (EPA), and the U.S. Department of Agriculture (USDA) have ethics rules for funded researchers.

Other influential research ethics policies include the Uniform Requirements for Manuscripts Submitted to Biomedical Journals (International Committee of Medical Journal Editors), the Chemist's Code of Conduct (American Chemical Society), Code of Ethics (American Society for Clinical Laboratory Science), Ethical Principles of Psychologists (American Psychological Association), Statements on Ethics and Professional Responsibility (American Anthropological Association), Statement on Professional Ethics (American Association of University Professors), the Nuremberg Code and the Declaration of Helsinki (World Medical Association).

3.5 UNESCO: Ethical Guidelines

1. Principal investigators.
2. Integrity of the research enterprise is maintained.
3. Potential benefit/harmful effects to the participants and society.
4. Consider the effects of his/her work, including the consequences or misuse.
5. Competent fashion.
6. Awareness of local customs, standards, laws and regulations.
7. Informed consent.
8. Potential participants should be informed about potentially harmful effects.
9. Full confidentiality.
10. Participants should be offered access to research results.
11. Reported widely.
12. Acknowledged.
13. Preserved.

3.6 Economic and Social Research Council (ESRC) UK—Guidelines

1. Research should be designed, reviewed and undertaken to ensure integrity and quality.
2. Research staff and subjects must be informed fully about the purpose, methods and intended possible uses of the research, what their participation in the research entails and what risks if any, are involved. Exceptionally, some variations may be acceptable.
3. The confidentiality of information supplied by research subjects and the anonymity of respondents must be respected.

4. Research participants must participate in a voluntary way, free from any coercion. Exceptionally, covert research and deception may be acceptable.
5. Harm to participants must be avoided. Avoidance of harm extends to family, kin, community groups should not be unreasonably excluded from research exceptionally, some limited short term and minimal harm may be acceptable.
6. The independence of the research must be clear; any conflicts of interest or partiality must be explicit.

3.7 APA Ethics Code Standard for Research and Publication

1. Institutional Approval.
2. Informed Consent to Research.
3. Informed Consent for Recording Voices and Images.
4. Client/Patient, Student, and Subordinate Research Participants.
5. Dispensing with Informed Consent.
6. Offering Inducements for Research Participation.
7. Deception in Research.
8. Debriefing.
9. Humane Care and Use of Animals in Research.
10. Reporting Research Results.
11. Plagiarism.
12. Publication Credit.
13. Duplicate Publication of Data.
14. Sharing Research for Verification.
15. Reviewers.

3.8 General Principles of Research Ethics

These actions would be regarded as unethical by most scientists and some might even be illegal. Most of these would also violate different professional ethics codes or institutional policies.

The following is a rough and general summary of some ethical principles that various codes address—

1. **Honesty**: Strive for honesty in all scientific communications. Honestly report data, results, methods and procedures, and publication status. Do not fabricate, falsify, or misrepresent data. Do not deceive colleagues, granting agencies, or the public.
2. **Objectivity**: Strive to avoid bias in experimental design, data analysis, data interpretation, peer review, personnel decisions, grant writing, expert testimony, and other aspects of research where objectivity is expected or required. Avoid or minimize bias or self-deception. Disclose personal or financial interests that may affect research.
3. **Integrity**: Keep your promises and agreements; act with sincerity; strive for consistency of thought and action.
4. **Carefulness**: Avoid careless errors and negligence; carefully and critically examine your own work and the work of your peers. Keep good records of research activities, such as data collection, research design, and correspondence with agencies or journals.
5. **Openness**: Share data, results, ideas, tools, resources. Be open to criticism and new ideas.
6. **Respect for Intellectual Property**: Honor patents, copyrights, and other forms of intellectual property. Do not use unpublished data, methods, or results without permission. Give credit where credit is due. Give proper acknowledgement or credit for all contributions to research. Never plagiarize.
7. **Confidentiality**: Protect confidential communications, such as papers or grants submitted for publication, personnel records, trade or military secrets, and patient records.
8. **Responsible Publication**: Publish in order to advance research and scholarship, not to advance just your own career. Avoid wasteful and duplicative publication.

9. **Responsible Mentoring:** Help to educate, mentor, and advise students. Promote their welfare and allow them to make their own decisions.
10. **Respect for Colleagues:** Respect your colleagues and treat them fairly.
11. **Social Responsibility:** Strive to promote social good and prevent or mitigate social harms through research, public education, and advocacy.
12. **Non-Discrimination:** Avoid discrimination against colleagues or students on the basis of sex, race, ethnicity, or other factors that are not related to their scientific competence and integrity.
13. **Competence:** Maintain and improve your own professional competence and expertise through lifelong education and learning; take steps to promote competence in science as a whole.
14. **Legality:** Know and obey relevant laws and institutional and governmental policies.
15. **Animal Care:** Show proper respect and care for animals when using them in research. Do not conduct unnecessary or poorly designed animal experiments.
16. **Human Subjects Protection:** When conducting research on human subjects minimize harms and risks and maximize benefits; respect human dignity, privacy, and autonomy; take special precautions with vulnerable populations; and strive to distribute the benefits and burdens of research fairly.

3.9 The 3 Rs of Research Ethics: Replacement, Reduction and Refinement

Encapsulated in the code of practice for the care and use of animals for scientific purposes is the requirement for scientific and teaching activities to consider the 3 Rs.

1. **Replacement**: Techniques that totally or partially replace the use of animals for scientific purposes must be sought and used wherever possible.
2. **Reduction**: Each project must use no more than the minimum number of animals necessary to ensure scientific and statistical validity. The principle of reducing the number of animals used should not be implemented at the expense of greater suffering of individual animals. Scientific and teaching activities involving the use of animals must not be repeated unless essential for the purpose or design of the project. Teaching activities must involve no more than the minimum number of animals required to reach the educational objectives. Overproduction of animals bred for scientific purposes should be avoided so that the need to kill healthy animals is minimized.
3. **Refinement**: Animals must be suitable for the scientific purpose taking into account their biological characteristics including behaviour, genetic attributes and nutritional, microbiological and general health status. The design and management of animal accommodation should meet with species-specific needs. Special consideration is required where this is precluded by the requirements of the project. Animals should be transported, housed, fed, watered, handled and used under conditions that meet species-specific needs.

3.10 Ethical Issues in Biological and Agricultural Research

1. **Sustainability**: Institutional capacities to address long term problems require different kinds of reinforcement than otherwise. Inter-species and inter-sector concerns also influence the sustainability of the outcomes. Not all local practices need to be sustained. Sustainability is as much about continuity as about discontinuity (that is innovations or fundamental change in values).

2. **Eco-system health:** When scientists know about the eco-system health and yet develop technologies which impair the health, they are not only making a trade-off but also passing a value judgment. Transferring costs of near term trade-offs over the longer term stakeholders may neither be ethical nor economically very judicious. Eco-system health is also affected when long term consequences of certain chemical inputs are known or anticipatable, and yet these are continued to be used. Judgments are involved when chemicals banned in Western countries are allowed to be used in developing countries, when the precautionary principle is applied or not applied, and while technologies are transferred to countries which may or may not have capacity to assess the consequences.
3. **Responsiveness:** In any context, not everybody's problem is equally important. Michael Lipton once drew attention to the biases that existed in favour of interesting pests' *vis-à-vis* the relevant ones. A good example is the cooking stove used by millions of women or carrying water pots on the head for long distance, transporting grass or twigs on head on the hill slopes by women or transplanting paddy by keeping feet under water and thus getting fungal infections etc.
4. **Accountability:** Researchers seldom share their findings with the people from whom they collect the data. Not only that they often do not even calibrate their criteria of relevant or not so relevant research by involving the users of research in calibration. The community of corporations has to evolve its own code of conduct censoring such behaviour.
5. **Capacity building:** Any society which has to grapple with risk and uncertainty inherent in agricultural resource management has to learn to create capacity not only to anticipate but also address the future problems. The education and training of young minds thus becomes a very important determinant of the capacity to face emerging challenges in future.

6. **Location specificity**: It is well known that agro-ecological environment in rainfed regions is much more heterogeneous. Developing technologies which would diffuse only in a small region poses an institutional challenge apart from technological challenge. When research infrastructure, allocation of human resources and priority in research are biased in favour of better endowed regions and communities, the ethics of neglecting the bypassed communities and regions has to be made explicit.
7. **Asymmetry in rights of and responsibilities towards knowledge holders**: No agricultural research council in developed or developing countries ever requires the asymmetry between rights and responsibilities towards the knowledge holders of informal sectors be deliberately overcome. The respondents in research with communities are not acknowledged, do not receive the findings of the research for which they provide data and do not receive any share in the benefits that are generated from the application or commercialization of the knowledge provided by the respondents/knowledge providers.
8. **Empowerment of informal innovators and knowledge holders**: Just as the scientists can generate a creative and innovative solution to a problem, a farmer or an artisan can too. The global bias against innovations in informal sector is very obvious. Inability of formal research system to listen to and learn from informal innovators not only deprives the organized sector of agricultural research and technology of the insights from the margin but also prevents from being inspired by the values of many of the grassroots innovators.

3.11 Research Misconduct

As per US Federal Policy "Research misconduct is defined as fabrication, falsification, or plagiarism in proposing, performing, or reviewing research, or in reporting research results."

It includes the potential cases of data fabrication, falsification, plagiarism, image manipulation, unethical research, biased reporting, authorship abuse, redundant or duplicate publication, and undeclared conflicts of interest.

3.12 Areas of Research Misconduct

- Plagiarism.
- Fabrication and falsification.
- Non-publication of data.
- Faulty data-gathering procedures.
- Poor data storage and retention.
- Misleading authorship.
- Sneaky publication practices.

Research misconduct means **Fabrication, Falsification**, or **Plagiarism (FFP)** in proposing, performing, or reviewing research, or in reporting research results.

(a) **Fabrication** is making up data or results and recording or reporting them.

(b) **Falsification** is manipulating research materials, equipment, or processes, or changing or omitting data or results such that the research is not accurately represented in the research record.

(c) **Plagiarism** is the appropriation of another person's ideas, processes, results, or words without giving appropriate credit.

Other Types of Ethical Violations

- Duplicate publication/submission of research findings; failure to inform the editor of related papers that the author has under consideration or "in press".

- Unrevealed conflicts of interest that could affect then interpretation of the findings.
- Misrepresentation of research findings—use of selective or fraudulent data to support a hypothesis or claim.

Source: http://ori.dhhs.gov/misconduct/definition_misconduct.sht

3.13 Other Deviations from Acceptable Research Practice

There are many other activities that do not define as "misconduct" but which are still regarded by most researchers as unethical. These are called "other deviations" from acceptable research practices and include:

1. Publishing the same paper in two different journals without telling the editors.
2. Submitting the same paper to different journals without telling the editors.
3. Not informing a collaborator of your intent to file a patent in order to make sure that you are the sole inventor.
4. Including a colleague as an author on a paper in return for a favour even though the colleague did not make a serious contribution to the paper.
5. Discussing with your colleagues confidential data from a paper that you are reviewing for a journal.
6. Trimming outliers from a data set without discussing your reasons in paper.
7. Using an inappropriate statistical technique in order to enhance the significance of your research.
8. Bypassing the peer review process and announcing your results through a press conference without giving peers adequate information to review your work.
9. Conducting a review of the literature that fails to acknowledge the contributions of other people in the field or relevant prior work.

10. Stretching the truth on a grant application in order to convince reviewers that your project will make a significant contribution to the field.
11. Stretching the truth on a job application or curriculum vitae.
12. Giving the same research project to two graduate students in order to see who can do it the fastest.
13. Overworking, neglecting, or exploiting graduate or post-doctoral students.
14. Failing to keep good research records.
15. Failing to maintain research data for a reasonable period of time.
16. Making derogatory comments and personal attacks in your review of author's submission.
17. Promising a student a better grade for sexual favours.
18. Using a racist epithet in the laboratory.
19. Making significant deviations from the research protocol approved by your institution's Animal Care and Use Committee or Institutional Review Board for Human Subjects Research without telling the committee or the board.
20. Not reporting an adverse event in a human research experiment.
21. Wasting animals in research.
22. Exposing students and staff to biological risks in violation of your institution's biosafety rules.
23. Rejecting a manuscript for publication without even reading it.
24. Sabotaging someone's work.
25. Stealing supplies, books, or data.
26. Rigging an experiment so you know how it will turn out.
27. Making unauthorized copies of data, papers, or computer programmes.
28. Deliberately overestimating the clinical significance of a new drug in order to obtain economic benefits.

3.14 Publication Ethics

Academic publishing depends, to a great extent, on trust. Editors trust peer reviewers to provide fair assessments, authors trust editors to select appropriate peer reviewers, and readers put their trust in the peer-review process. Academic publishing also occurs in an environment of powerful intellectual, financial, and sometimes political interests that may collide or compete.

Ethical standards for publication exist to ensure high-quality scientific publications, public trust in scientific findings, and that people receive credit for their work and ideas.

It is important to avoid any violation in the ethics related to publication.

3.15 Violation of Publication Ethics

1. Data Fabrication and Falsification

Data fabrication means the researcher did not actually do the study, but made up data. Data falsification means the researcher did the experiment, but then changed some of the data. Both of these practices make people distrust scientists. If the public is mistrustful of science then it will be less willing to provide funding support.

2. Plagiarism

Taking the ideas and work of others without giving them credit is unfair and dishonest. Copying even one sentence from someone else's manuscript, or even one of your own that has previously been published, without proper citation is considered plagiarism—use your own words instead.

3. Image Manipulation

Changes to images can create misleading results when research data are collected as images. Thus inappropriate image manipulation is one form of fabrication or falsification that journals can identify.

It may, however, be legitimate and even necessary to edit images. For example, the selective enlargement of part of an artwork may be needed to reveal features that would not otherwise be visible, and editing of video data may be needed to protect the privacy of participants.

4. Multiple Submissions

It is unethical to submit the same manuscript to more than one journal at the same time. Doing this wastes the time of editors and peer reviewers, and can damage the reputation of journals if published in more than one. If authors have used their own previously published work, or work that is currently under review, as the basis for a submitted manuscript, they must cite the previous articles and indicate how their submitted manuscript differs from their previous work. Reuse of the authors' own words outside the Methods should be attributed or quoted in the text. Reuse of the authors' own figures or substantial amounts of wording may require permission from the copyright holder and the authors are responsible for obtaining this.

5. Redundant Publication (Salami Slicing)

Redundant publication, the inappropriate division of study outcomes into more than one article (also known as salami slicing), may result in rejection or a request to merge submitted manuscripts, and the correction of published articles. Duplicate publication of the same, or a very similar article may result in the retraction of the later article and the authors may incur sanctions.

6. Citation Manipulation

Authors whose submitted manuscripts are found to include citations whose primary purpose is to increase the number of citations to a given author's work, or to articles published in a particular journal, may incur sanctions.

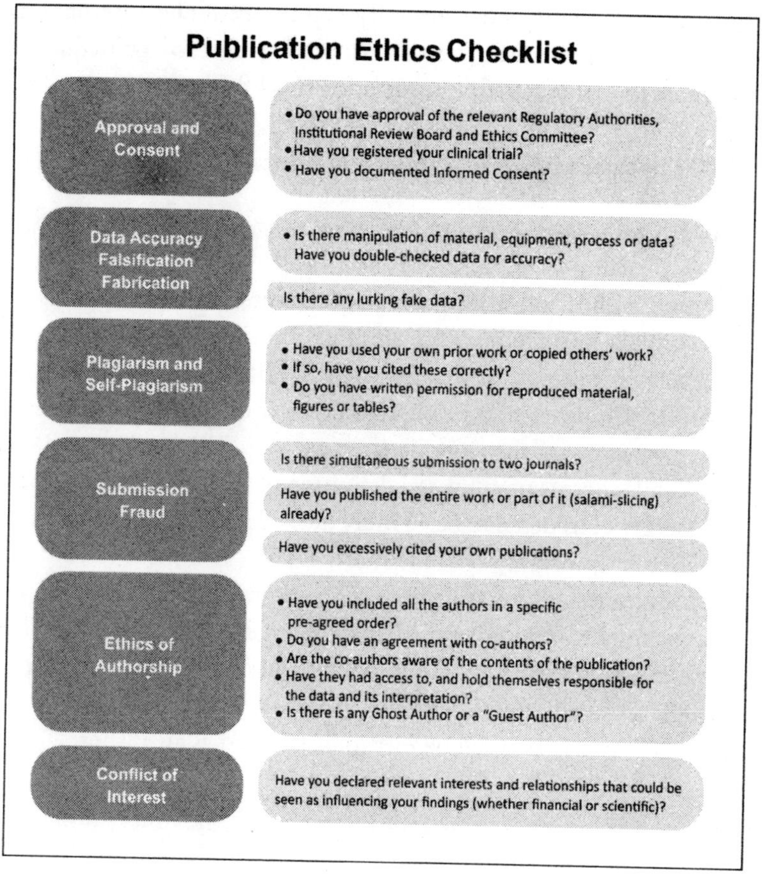

Image courtesy: Indian Journal of Ophthalmology.

Editors and reviewers must not ask authors to include references merely to increase citations to their own or an associate's work, to the journal, or to another journal they are associated with.

7. Improper Author Contribution or Attribution

All listed authors must have made a significant scientific contribution to the research in the manuscript and approved all its claims. Do not forget to list everyone who made a significant scientific contribution, including students and laboratory technicians. The International Committee of Medical Journal Editors has detailed guidelines on authorship that are useful for scientists in all fields.

3.16 Important Issues of Publication Ethics

3.16.1 Authorship and Collaborative Research

Naming authors on a scientific paper ensures that the appropriate individuals get credit, and are accountable, for the research. Deliberately misrepresenting a scientist's relationship to their work is considered to be a form of misconduct that undermines confidence in the reporting of the work itself.

While there is no universal definition of authorship, an "author" is generally considered to be an individual who has made a significant intellectual contribution to the study.

According to the guidelines for authorship established by the International Committee of Medical Journal Editors (ICMJE), "All persons designated as authors should qualify for authorship, and all those who qualify should be listed."

Four criteria must all be met to be credited as an author:

- Substantial contribution to the study conception and design, data acquisition, analysis, and interpretation.
- Drafting or revising the article for intellectual content.
- Approval of the final version.
- Agreement to be accountable for all aspects of the work related to the accuracy or integrity of any part of the work.

The following are some general guidelines, which may vary from field to field:

The order of authorship should be "a joint decision of the co-authors".

Individuals who are involved in a study but don't satisfy the journal's criteria for authorship, should be listed as "Contributors" or "Acknowledged Individuals".

Examples include: assisting the research by providing advice, providing research space, departmental oversight, and obtaining financial support.

For large, multi-centre trials, the list of clinicians and centres is typically published, along with a statement of the individual contributions made.

Some groups list authors alphabetically, sometimes with a note to explain that all authors made equal contributions to the study and the publication.

Three types of authorship are considered unacceptable:

- "Ghost" authors, who contribute substantially but are not acknowledged (often paid by commercial sponsors); This usually refers to professional writers (one paid by commercial sponsors) whose role is not acknowledged. Unattributed contributions to data analyses may also constitute ghost authorship.
- "Guest" authors, who make no discernible contributions, but are listed to help increase the chances of publication; Authorship based on an expectation that inclusion of a particular name will improve the chances that the study will be published.
- "Gift" authors, whose contribution is based solely on a tenuous affiliation with a study.

When not appropriately addressed, authorship issues can lead to dispute. Some disputes are based on misconduct (such as lying about one's role); some stem from questions of interpretation, such as the degree to which a person's contribution can be considered "substantial", and if authorship is justified.

Other potential issues could include: being involved in a study, but not listed as an author or contributor; someone taking your idea and publishing a paper claiming full authorship; and finding your name on a publication without your permission.

If a complaint is filed over a dispute, an investigation may be conducted with the journal editor and author's institution to reach a resolution. Because of the potential for ambiguity and confused expectations, it is strongly advised that before the research begins, a meeting take place to document how each person will be acknowledged.

Issues around authorship can be complex and sensitive. Early career researchers who encounter such situations may fear they will jeopardize their reputation and career if they speak up. Take the time to fully understand each journal's guidelines for authorship, and industry requirements. If you find yourself in a challenging situation that you are not sure how to handle, consult with a trusted mentor or supervisor.

3.16.2 Conflict of Interest and Commitment

When an investigator, author, editor, or reviewer has a financial/personal interest or belief that could affect his/her objectivity, or inappropriately influence his/her actions, a potential competing interest exists. Such relationships are also known as dual commitments, competing interests, or competing loyalties.

The most obvious competing interests are financial relationships such as:

Direct: employment, stock ownership, grants, patents.

Indirect: honoraria, consultancies to sponsoring organizations, mutual fund ownership, paid expert testimony.

Undeclared financial interests may seriously undermine the credibility of the journal, the authors, and the science itself. An example might be an investigator who owns stock in a pharmaceutical company that is commissioning the research.

Competing interests can also exist as a result of personal relationships, academic competition, and intellectual passion.

An example might be a researcher who has:

- A relative who works at the company whose product the researcher is evaluating.
- A self-serving stake in the research results (e.g. potential promotion/career advancement based on outcomes).
- Personal beliefs that are in direct conflict with the topic he/she is researching.

Not all relationships represent a true competing interest—conflicts can be potential or actual. Some considerations that should be taken into account include: whether the person's association with the organization interferes with their ability to carry out the research or paper without bias; and whether the relationship, when later revealed, make a reasonable reader feel deceived or misled.

Conflicts include the following:

Financial—funding and other payments, goods and services received or expected by the authors relating to the subject of the work or from an organization with an interest in the outcome of the work.

Affiliations—being employed by, on the advisory board for, or a member of an organization with an interest in the outcome of the work.

Intellectual property—patents or trademarks owned by someone or their organization.

Personal—friends, family, relationships, and other close personal connections.

Ideology—beliefs or activism, for example, political or religious, relevant to the work.

Academic—competitors or someone whose work is critiqued.

Full disclosure about a relationship that could constitute a competing interest—even if the person does not believe it affects their judgment—should be reported to the institution's ethics group and to the journal editor to which a paper is submitted. Most publishers require disclosure in the form of a cover letter and/or footnote in the manuscript.

Typical form to capture conflicts of interest during manuscri pt submission

Conflict of Interest

This publication requires that all authors disclose any potential sources of conflict of interest. An interest or relationship, financial or otherwise, that might be perceived as influencing an author's objectivity is considered a potential source of conflict of interest. These must be disclosed when directly relevant or indirectly related to the work that the authors describe in their manuscript. Potential sources of conflict of interest include but are not limited to patent or stock ownership, membership of a company board of directions, membership of an advisory board or committee for a company, and consultancy for or receipt of speaker's fees from a company. The existence of a conflict of interest does not prelude publication in this journal.

If the authors have no conflict of interest to declare, they must also state this at submission. It is the responsibility of the corresponding author to review this policy with all authors and to collectively list in the cover letter (if applicable) to the Editor-in-Chief, in the manuscript (in the footnotes, Conflict of Interest or Acknowledgment section), and in the online submission system All pertinent commercial and other relationships.

req Do you or any of your co-authors have a conflict of interest to declare?

Yes

No

Confirm that you have stated this conflict of interest in the footnotes, Conflict of Interest or Acknowledgments section of you manuscript as required by the Journal (see the Instructions to Authors.)

(Confirmed)

Provide details and include this information below.

Image courtesy: WILEY Guidelines for Publication Ethics.

A journal may use disclosures as a basis for editorial decisions and will publish them as they may be important to readers in judging the manuscript. Likewise, the journal may decide not to publish on the basis of the declared conflict.

According to the U.S. Office of Research Integrity, having a competing interest is not in itself unethical, and there are some that are unavoidable. Full transparency is always the best course of action, and, if in doubt, disclose.

3.17 Committee on Publication Ethics (COPE) Guidelines on Good Publication Practice

COPE was founded in 1997 to address breaches of research and publication ethics. A voluntary body providing a discussion forum and advice for scientific editors, it aims to find practical ways of dealing with the issues, and to develop good practice.

We thought it essential to attempt to define best practice in the ethics of scientific publishing. These guidelines should be useful for authors, editors, editorial board members, readers, owners of journals, and publishers. Intellectual honesty should be actively encouraged in all medical and scientific courses of study, and used to inform publication ethics and prevent misconduct. It is with that in mind that these guidelines have been produced.

The guidelines were developed from a preliminary version drafted by individual members of the committee, which was then submitted to extensive consultation. They address: study design and ethical approval, data analysis, authorship, conflict of interests, the peer review process, redundant publication, plagiarism, duties of editors, media relations, advertising, and how to deal with misconduct.

These guidelines are intended to be advisory rather than prescriptive, and to evolve over time. We hope that they will be disseminated widely, endorsed by editors, and refined by those who use them.

1. Study Design and Ethical Approval

Definition

Good research should be well justified, well planned, appropriately designed, and ethically approved. To conduct research to a lower standard may constitute misconduct.

Action

(1) Laboratory and clinical research should be driven by protocol; pilot studies should have a written rationale.

(2) Research protocols should seek to answer specific questions, rather than just collect data.

(3) Protocols must be carefully agreed by all contributors and collaborators, including, if appropriate, the participants.

(4) The final protocol should form part of the research record.

(5) Early agreement on the precise roles of the contributors and collaborators, and on matters of authorship and publication, is advised.

(6) Statistical issues should be considered early in study design, including power calculations, to ensure there are neither too few nor too many participants.

(7) Formal and documented ethical approval from an appropriately constituted research ethics committee is required for all studies involving people, medical records, and anonymised human tissues.

(8) Use of human tissues in research should conform to the highest ethical standards, such as those recommended by the Nuffield Council on Bioethics.

(9) Fully informed consent should always be sought. It may not always be possible, however, and in such circumstances, an appropriately constituted research ethics committee should decide if this is ethically acceptable.

(10) When participants are unable to give fully informed consent, research should follow international guidelines, such as those of the Council for International Organizations of Medical Sciences (CIOMS).

(11) Animal experiments require full compliance with local, national, ethical, and regulatory principles, and local licensing arrangements. International standards vary.

(12) Formal supervision, usually the responsibility of the principal investigator, should be provided for all research projects: this must include quality control, and the frequent review and long term retention (may be up to 15 years) of all records and primary outputs.

2. Data Analysis

Definition

Data should be appropriately analysed, but inappropriate analysis does not necessarily amount to misconduct. Fabrication and falsification of data do constitute misconduct.

Action

(1) All sources and methods used to obtain and analyse data, including any electronic pre-processing, should be fully disclosed; detailed explanations should be provided for any exclusion.

(2) Methods of analysis must be explained in detail, and referenced, if they are not in common use.

(3) The post hoc analysis of subgroups is acceptable, as long as this is disclosed. Failure to disclose that the analysis was post hoc is unacceptable.

(4) The discussion section of a paper should mention any issues of bias which have been considered, and explain how they have been dealt with in the design and interpretation of the study.

3. Authorship

Definition

There is no universally agreed definition of authorship, although attempts have been made (see Appendix). As a minimum, authors should take responsibility for a particular section of the study.

Action

(1) The award of authorship should balance intellectual contributions to the conception, design, analysis and writing of the study against the collection of data and other routine work. If there is no task that can reasonably be attributed to a particular individual, then that individual should not be credited with authorship.

(2) To avoid disputes over attribution of academic credit, it is helpful to decide early on in the planning of a research project who will be credited as authors, as contributors, and who will be acknowledged.

(3) All authors must take public responsibility for the content of their paper. The multidisciplinary nature of much research can make this difficult, but this can be resolved by the disclosure of individual contributions.

(4) Careful reading of the target journal's "Advice to Authors" is advised, in the light of current uncertainties.

4. Conflicts of Interest

Definition

Conflicts of interest comprise those which may not be fully apparent and which may influence the judgment of authors, reviewers and editors.

They have been described as those which, when revealed later, would make a reasonable reader feel misled or deceived.

They may be personal, commercial, political, academic or financial. "Financial" interests may include employment, research funding, stock or share ownership, payment for lectures or travel, consultancies and company support for staff.

Action

(1) Such interests, where relevant, must be declared to editors by researchers, authors, and reviewers.

(2) Editors should also disclose relevant conflicts of interest to their readers. If in doubt, disclose.

Sometimes editors may need to withdraw from the review and selection process for the relevant submission.

5. Peer Review

Definition

Peer reviewers are external experts chosen by editors to provide written opinions, with the aim of improving the study.

Working methods vary from journal to journal, but some use open procedures in which the name of the reviewer is disclosed, together with the full or "edited" report.

Action

(1) Suggestions from authors as to who might act as reviewers are often useful, but there should be no obligation on editors to use those suggestions.

(2) The duty of confidentiality in the assessment of a manuscript must be maintained by expert reviewers, and this extends to reviewers' colleagues who may be asked (with the editor's permission) to give opinions on specific sections.

(3) The submitted manuscript should not be retained or copied.

(4) Reviewers and editors should not make any use of the data, arguments, or interpretations, unless they have the authors' permission.

(5) Reviewers should provide speedy, accurate, courteous, unbiased and justifiable reports.

(6) If reviewers suspect misconduct, they should write in confidence to the editor.

(7) Journals should publish accurate descriptions of their peer review, selection, and appeals processes.

(8) Journals should also provide regular audits of their acceptance rates and publication times.

6. Redundant Publication

Definition

Redundant publication occurs when two or more papers, without full cross-reference, share the same hypothesis, data, discussion points, or conclusions.

Action

(1) Published studies do not need to be repeated unless further confirmation is required.

(2) Previous publication of an abstract during the proceedings of meetings does not preclude subsequent submission for publication, but full disclosure should be made at the time of submission.

(3) Re-publication of a paper in another language is acceptable, provided that there is full and prominent disclosure of its original source at the time of submission.

(4) At the time of submission, authors should disclose details of related papers, even if in a different language, and similar papers in press.

7. Plagiarism

Definition

Plagiarism ranges from the unreferenced use of others published and unpublished ideas, including research grant applications to submission under "new" authorship of a complete paper, sometimes in a different language.

It may occur at any stage of planning, research, writing, or publication: it applies to print and electronic versions.

Action

(1) All sources should be disclosed, and if large amounts of other people's written or illustrative materials are to be used, permission must be sought.

8. Duties of Editors

Definition

Editors are the stewards of journals. They usually take over their journal from the previous editor(s) and always want to hand over the journal in good shape.

Most editors provide direction for the journal and build a strong management team.

They must consider and balance the interests of many constituents, including readers, authors, staff, owners, editorial board members, advertisers and the media.

Actions

(1) Editors' decisions to accept or reject a paper for publication should be based only on the paper's importance, originality, and clarity, and the study's relevance to the merit of the journal.

(2) Studies that challenge previous work published in the journal should be given an especially sympathetic hearing.

(3) Studies reporting negative results should not be excluded.

(4) All original studies should be peer reviewed before publication, taking into full account possible bias due to related or conflicting interests.

(5) Editors must treat all submitted papers as confidential.

(6) When a published paper is subsequently found to contain major flaws, editors must accept responsibility for correcting the record prominently and promptly.

9. Media Relations

Definition

Medical research findings are of increasing interest to the print and broadcast media.

Journalists may attend scientific meetings at which preliminary research findings are presented, leading to their premature publication in the mass media.

Action

(1) Authors approached by the media should give as balanced an account of their work as possible, ensuring that they point out where evidence ends and speculation begins.

(2) Simultaneous publication in the mass media and a peer reviewed journal is advised, as this usually means that enough evidence and data have been provided to satisfy informed and critical readers.

(3) Where this is not possible, authors should help journalists to produce accurate reports, but refrain from supplying additional data.

(4) All efforts should be made to ensure that patient who has helped with the research should be informed of the results by the authors before the mass media, especially if there are clinical implications.

(5) Authors should be advised by the organisers if journalists are to attend scientific meetings.

(6) It may be helpful to authors to be advised of any media policies operated by the journal in which their work is to be published.

10. Advertising

Definition

Many scientific journals and meetings derive significant income from advertising. Reprints may also be lucrative.

Action

(1) Editorial decisions must not be influenced by advertising revenue or reprint potential: editorial and advertising administration must be clearly separated.

(2) Advertisements that mislead must be refused, and editors must be willing to publish criticisms, according to the same criteria used for material in the rest of the journal.

(3) Reprints should be published as they appear in the journal unless a correction is to be added.

3.18 Some Examples of Ethical Violations in Research and Publication

Example 1: Violations in Research and Publication Ethics

24 MAY 2002 VOL 296 SCIENCE, p 1376

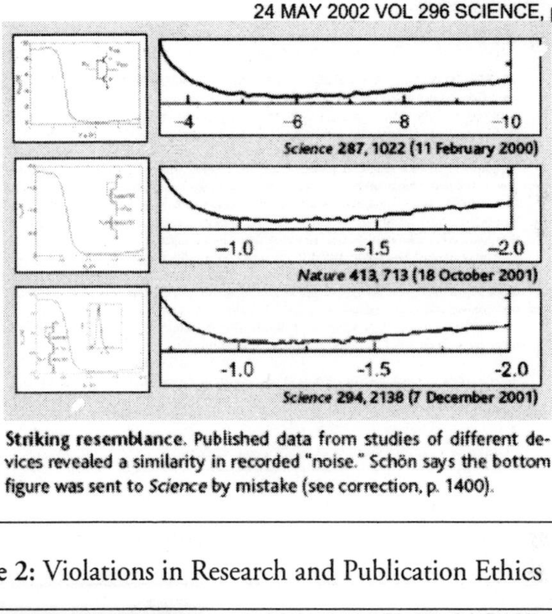

Striking resemblance. Published data from studies of different devices revealed a similarity in recorded "noise." Schön says the bottom figure was sent to *Science* by mistake (see correction, p. 1400).

Example 2: Violations in Research and Publication Ethics

RESEARCH INTEGRITY 24 MAY 2002 VOL 296 SCIENCE, p 1376

Pioneering Physics Papers Under Suspicion for Data Manipulation

Recent discoveries at Bell Laboratories—the research arm of Lucent Technologies in Murray Hill, New Jersey—said to be of Nobel quality suddenly became mired in questions last week. Outside researchers presented evidence to Bell Labs management on 10 May suggesting possible manipulation of data involving five papers published in *Science*, *Nature*, and *Applied Physics Letters* over 2 years. In response, Bell Labs officials said that they are forming a committee of independent researchers to investigate. Their conclusions may not be known for months, but scientists who have seen the data are already saying that the potential fallout from the investigation could be devastating.

The Bell Labs papers describe a series of different experiments with organic conduc- Angeles, and director of the California NanoSystems Institute: "It's hard to understand. I know these people. Most of them are good, careful scientists." "It's a little overwhelming," adds Lydia Sohn, a Princeton University physicist who helped bring some of the discrepancies to light. "It's just disturbing, and disappointing, and sad." The noise pattern is particularly disturbing, says Charles Lieber, a chemist and nanoscience expert at Harvard University in Cambridge, Massachusetts: "It's virtually impossible for me to believe that some of this wasn't made up."

Schön himself acknowledges that the similar noise pattern is "difficult to explain." But others affiliated with Bell Labs suggest privately that a systematic artifact in the measurement equipment might account for

Example 3: Violations in Research and Publication Ethics

Science 27 JULY 2007 VOL 317 SCIENCE www.sciencemag.org

Retraction

WE WISH TO RETRACT OUR REPORT "*CDX2* GENE EXPRESSION AND TROPHECTODERM LINEAGE specification in mouse embryos" (*1*). Allegations of research misconduct were received by the University of Missouri-Columbia (MU) Provost, and an investigation found that the first author (K.D.) engaged in research misconduct by intentionally falsifying and fabricating digital images in the preparation of Figs. 4I; 4N; 4S; 2G; 3, J to L; S2, V to X; and S6, I to K accompanying the *Science* article. In addition, the original raw image files for the majority of the figures in the paper have not been located (the exceptions being the confocal scanning images in Figs. S1, S3, S4, S5, and S6), raising the possibility that the data they represent may also be suspect. We have decided to withdraw the article in its entirety in view of the fact that the paper was founded at least in part on falsified or fabricated images.

The corresponding author (R.M.R.) takes responsibility for placing excessive trust in his co-worker and for not assuring that a complete set of raw data existed at the time the questions first arose about the paper. We deeply regret any scientific misconceptions that have resulted from the publication of this article.

The first author resigned from MU shortly after the allegations of research misconduct were received and could not be found to sign the retraction.

R. MICHAEL ROBERTS,[1] M. SIVAGURU,[2] H. Y. YONG[3]

[1]Division of Animal Sciences, University of Missouri, Columbia, MO 65211, USA. [2]Institute for Genomic Biology, University of Illinois, Urbana-Champaign, IL 61801, USA. [3]BK21 Dental Research Institute, College of Dentistry, Seoul National University, 28 Yongun-dong, Chongno-gu, Seoul 110-749, Korea.

Reference

1. K. Deb, M. Sivaguru, H. Y. Yong, R. M. Roberts, *Science* 311, 992 (2006).

Example 4: Violations in Research and Publication Ethics

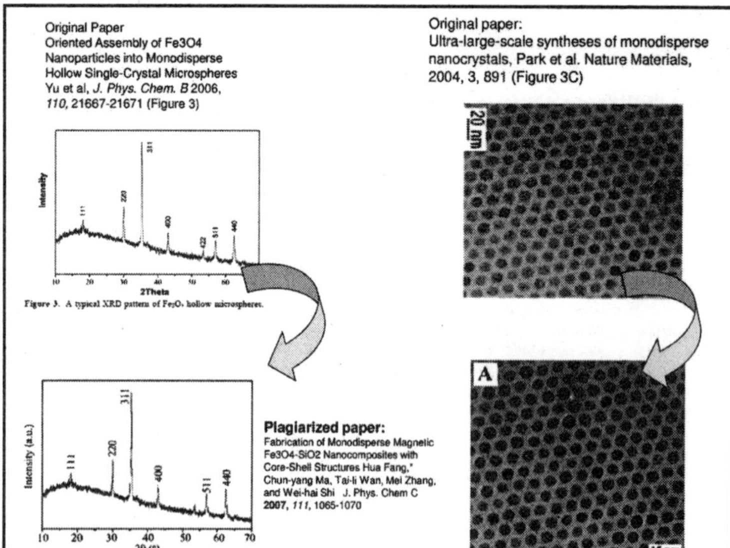

Example 5: Violations in Research and Publication Ethics

Paper trail reveals references go unread by citing authors

Philip Ball

Many of the references cited in scientific papers have not been read by the authors citing them, according to an analysis of how errors in citations propagate through the literature.

It isn't easy to establish directly — and truthfully — whether citations have been reference being copied from someone else's citation list. The most common misprint appeared 78 times.

Based on the number of distinct misprints, the two researchers estimate that only 22–23% of citations followed from a reading of the original paper. And they postulate that this is typical of the scientific literature as a whole.

NATURE|VOL 420 | 12 DECEMBER 2002, p. 594

Examples 6 and 7: Violations in Research and Publication Ethics

RETRACTED: Fluorescence lifetime increase by introduction of F^- ions in ytterbium-doped TeO_2-based glasses
Journal of Alloys and Compounds, Volume 393, Issues 1-2, 3 May 2005, Pages 279-282
Guonian Wang, Shixun Dai, Junjie Zhang, Shiqing Xu and Zhonghong Jiang

RETRACTED

RETRACTED: Effect of F− ions on spectroscopic properties of Yb^{3+}-doped zinc–tellurite glasses •
Journal of Physics and Chemistry of Solids, Volume 66, Issue 6, June 2005, Pages 1107-1111
Guonian Wang, Junjie Zhang, Shixun Dai, Jianhu Yang and Zhonghong Jiang

From Science@Direct (Elsevier)

SCIENTIFIC INTEGRITY

SCIENCE VOL 323 6 MARCH 2009, p1293

Responding to Possible Plagiarism

Documenting reactions from authors and journal editors to plagiarism may help others address the problem.

Tara C. Long,[1] Mounir Errami,[2] Angela C. George,[1] Zhaohui Sun,[2] Harold R. Garner[1,2*]

212 pairs of articles with signs of potential plagiarism were chosen for this study

86.2% -similarity between an original article and its duplicate

73.1%. the average number of shared references

Only 47 (22.2%) duplicates cited the original article as a reference.

71.4% of the manuscript pairs shared at least one highly similar or identical table or figure.

42% also contained incorrect calculations, data inconsistencies, and reproduced or manipulated photographs.

....The increasing availability of scientific literature on the World Wide Web has proven to be a double-edged sword, allowing plagiarism to be more easily committed, while simultaneously enabling its simple detection through the use of automated software.

Example 8: Violations in Research and Publication Ethics

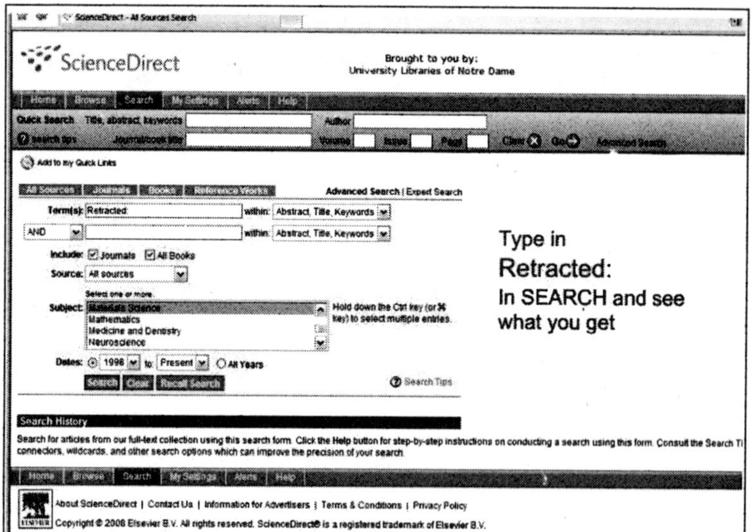

http://www.sciencedirect.com/science?_ob=MiamiSearchURL&_method=requestForm&_btn=Y&_acct=C000022718&_version=1&_urlVersion=1&_userid=489835&md5=ea66227488401c79ca7231fece33c1f4

Example 9: Violations in Research and Publication Ethics

Science AAAS

*Science***Insider**

Breaking news and analysis from the world of science policy

July 28, 2009

Journal Editor Retracts Paper on Sperm Made From Stem Cells

The paper, published online by ***Stem Cells and Development*** **on 8 July with Karim Nayernia of Newcastle University in the United Kingdom** as the corresponding author, had already received some criticism from other experts; Dr Allan Pacey of the University of Sheffield in the United Kingdom, for example, was quoted by *The Independent* as saying: "As a sperm biologist of 20 years' experience, I am unconvinced from the data presented in this paper that the cells produced ... can be accurately called 'Spermatozoa.' "

The paper's problems soon got much worse. Graham Parker, editor-in-chief of *Stem Cells and Development*, told *Science*Insider that he received an email on 10 July from the editors of another journal, *Biology of Reproduction*, claiming that **two paragraphs from Nayernia paper's introduction were copied without attribution from a** 2007 review article by Makoto Nagano of McGill University in Montreal, Canada, that was published in their journal.

Parker says Nayernia told him the offending text was inserted by a postdoctoral fellow. But Parker says the explanation he received was not consistent with an innocent mistake. "Once I had established that the suggested reason for the text's inclusion was not being substantiated I decided to retract the paper" on 21 July, Parker says.

Example 10: Violations in Research and Publication Ethics

C&EN
CHEMICAL & ENGINEERING NEWS

Home | Current Issue | Features | Alerts | Careers | Multimedia | Archive

Home » Science & Technology » **A Massive Case Of Fraud**

SCIENCE / **TECHNOLOGY**

FEBRUARY 18, 2008 | VOLUME 86, NUMBER 07 | PP. 37-38

A Massive Case Of Fraud

Journal editors are left reeling as publishers move to rid their archives of scientist's falsified research

William G. Schulz

A CHEMIST IN INDIA has been found guilty of plagiarizing and/or falsifying more than 70 research papers published in a wide variety of Western scientific journals between 2004 and 2007, according to documents from his university, copies of which were obtained by C&EN. Some journal editors left reeling by the incident say it is one of the most spectacular and outrageous cases of scientific fraud they have ever seen.

The culprit, sources say, is chemistry professor Pattium Chiranjeevi of Sri Venkateswara University in Tirupati, India. SVU conducted an investigation into Chiranjeevi's work after a journal editor presented evidence to university officials that the professor had plagiarized and possibly falsified several manuscript submissions. Chiranjeevi, who communicates through a wide variety of e-mail addresses, has not responded to multiple requests for comment by C&EN.

Chiranjeevi retains his teaching position at SVU, according to a university source who has requested anonymity. "He is a permanent employee of the university, and the administration cannot fire him easily," the source says. Instead, Chiranjeevi has been barred from research and research supervision and from holding any administrative post at the university.

A CHEMIST IN INDIA has been found guilty of plagiarizing and/or falsifying more than 70 research papers published in a wide variety of Western scientific journals between 2004 and 2007, according to documents from his university, copies of which were obtained by C&CN. Some journal editors left reeling by the incident say it is one of the most spectacular and outrageous cases of scientific fraud they have ever seen.

Example 11: Violations in Research and Publication Ethics

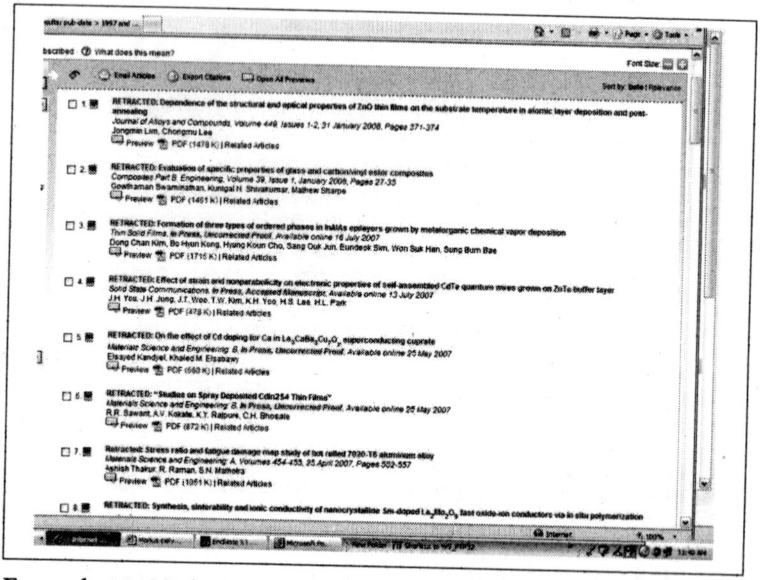

Example 12: Violations in Research and Publication Ethics

SCIENCE VOL 323 6 MARCH 2009, p.1293

There are now dozens of commercial and free tools available for the detection of plagiarism.

Perhaps the most popular programs are iParadigm's "Ithenticate" (http://ithenticate.com/) and TurnItIn's originality checking (http://turnitin.com/), which recently partnered with CrossRef (http://www.crossref.org/) to create CrossCheck, a new service for verifying the originality of scholarly content.

However, the content searched by this program spans only a small sampling of journals indexed by MEDLINE.

PubMed and other searches which, by default, return more recent articles first, ensuring that a plagiarized article will always appear higher on a list of search results than its original counterpart. As a result, citations that would have otherwise gone to an original publication are instead diverted to a plagiarized one.

Example 13: Violations in Research and Publication Ethics

Mounir Errami & Harold Garner
Nature **451**, 397-399 (24 Jan 2008)

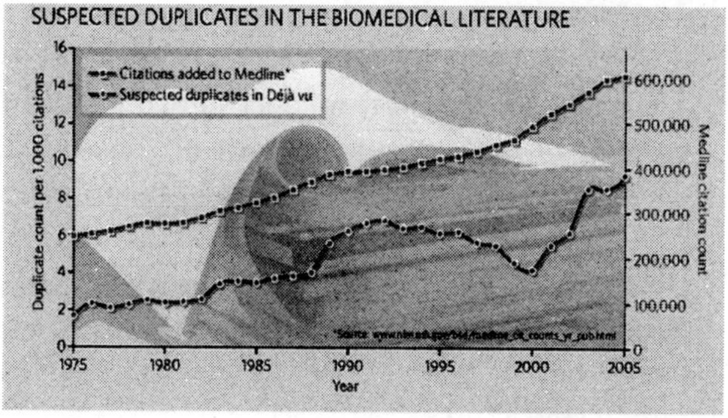

Example 14: Violations in Research and Publication Ethics

SCIENTIFIC INTEGRITY

SCIENCE VOL 323 6 MARCH 2009, p.1293

Responding to Possible Plagiarism

Documenting reactions from authors and journal editors to plagiarism may help others address the problem.

Tara C. Long,[1] Mounir Errami,[2] Angela C. George,[1] Zhaohui Sun,[2] Harold R. Garner[1,2*]

The responses from duplicate authors were more varied;

- 28% denied any wrongdoing.
- 35% admitted to having borrowed previously published material.
- 22% were from coauthors claiming no involvement in the writing of the manuscript.
- 17% claimed they were unaware that their names appeared on the article.

93% of the original authors were not aware of the duplicate's existence.

The journal editors primarily confirmed receipt and addressed issues involving policies and potential actions.

Source of example Images: Prashant V. Kamat slides (slideshare.net)

3.19 COPE Guidelines to Deal with Misconduct

1. Principles

(1) The general principle confirming misconduct is intention to cause others to regard as true that which is not true.
(2) The examination of misconduct must therefore focus, not only on the particular act or omission, but also on the intention of the researcher, author, editor, reviewer or publisher involved.
(3) Deception may be by intention, by reckless disregard of possible consequences, or by negligence. It is implicit, therefore, that "best practice" requires complete honesty, with full disclosure.
(4) Codes of practice may raise awareness, but can never be exhaustive.

2. Investigating Misconduct

(1) Editors should not simply reject papers that raise questions of misconduct. They are ethically obliged to pursue the case. However, knowing how to investigate and respond to possible cases of misconduct is difficult.
(2) COPE is always willing to advise, but for legal reasons, can only advise on anonymised cases.
(3) It is for the editor to decide what action to take.

3. Serious Misconduct

(1) Editors must take all allegations and suspicions of misconduct seriously, but they must recognise that they do not usually have either the legal legitimacy or the means to conduct investigations into serious cases.
(2) The editor must decide when to alert the employers of the accused author(s).

(3) Some evidence is required, but if employers have a process for investigating accusations—as they are increasingly required to do—then editors do not need to assemble a complete case. Indeed, it may be ethically unsound for editors to do so, because such action usually means consulting experts, so spreading abroad serious questions about the author(s).

(4) If editors are presented with convincing evidence—perhaps by reviewers—of serious misconduct, they should immediately pass this on to the employers, notifying the author(s) that they are doing so.

(5) If accusations of serious misconduct are not accompanied by convincing evidence, then editors should confidentially seek expert advice.

(6) If the experts raise serious questions about the research, then editors should notify the employers.

(7) If the experts find no evidence of misconduct, the editorial processes should proceed in the normal way.

(8) If presented with convincing evidence of serious misconduct, where there is no employer to whom this can be referred, and the author(s) are registered doctors, cases can be referred to the General Medical Council.

(9) If, however, there is no organisation with the legitimacy and the means to conduct an investigation, then the editor may decide that the case is sufficiently important to warrant publishing something in the journal. Legal advice will then be essential.

(10) If editors are convinced that an employer has not conducted an adequate investigation of a serious accusation, they may feel that publication of a notice in the journal is warranted. Legal advice will be essential.

(11) Authors should be given the opportunity to respond to accusations of serious misconduct.

4. Less Serious Misconduct

(1) Editors may judge that it is not necessary to involve employers in less serious cases of misconduct, such as redundant publication, deception over authorship, or failure to declare conflict of interest. Sometimes, the evidence may speak for itself, although it may be wise to appoint an independent expert.

(2) Editors should remember that accusations of even minor misconduct may have serious implications for the author(s), and it may then be necessary to ask the employers to investigate.

(3) Authors should be given the opportunity to respond to any charge of minor misconduct.

(4) If convinced of wrongdoing, editors may wish to adopt some of the sanctions outlined below.

5. Sanctions

Sanctions may be applied separately or combined. The following are ranked in approximate order of severity:

(1) A letter of explanation (and education) to the authors, where there appears to be a genuine misunderstanding of principles.

(2) A letter of reprimand and warning as to future conduct.

(3) A formal letter to the relevant head of institution or funding body.

(4) Publication of a notice of redundant publication or plagiarism.

(5) An editorial giving full details of the misconduct.

(6) Refusal to accept future submissions from the individual, unit, or institution responsible for the misconduct, for a stated period.

(7) Formal withdrawal or retraction of the paper from the scientific literature, informing other editors and the indexing authorities.
(8) Reporting the case to the General Medical Council, or other such authority or organisation which can investigate and act with due process.

3.20 Predatory Journal

A predatory journal is a publication that actively asks researchers for manuscripts. They have no peer review system and no true editorial board and are often found to publish mediocre or even worthless papers. They also ask for huge publication charges.

3.20.1 Beall's Criteria for Identification of Predatory Journals and Publishers

(1) No single individual is identified as specific journal's editor with no formal editorial/review board or the same editorial board for more than one journal.
(2) The editor and/or review board members do not have academic expertise in the journal's field.
(3) Provides insufficient information or hides information about author's fees, offering to publish an author's paper and later sending an unanticipated 'surprise' invoice.
(4) No proper indexing.
(5) The name of a journal is unrelated with the journal's mission.
(6) The name of a journal does not adequately reflect its origin (e.g. a journal with the word 'Canadian' or 'Swiss' in its name when neither the publisher, editor, nor any purported institutional affiliate relates whatsoever to Canada or Switzerland).
(7) The publisher has poorly maintained websites, including dead links, prominent misspellings and grammatical errors on the website.

(8) The publisher makes unauthorised use of licensed images on their website, taken from the open web, without permission or licensing from the copyright owners.
(9) Re-publish papers already published in other venues/outlets without providing appropriate credits.
(10) Use boastful language claiming to be a 'leading publisher' even though the publisher may only be a start-up or a novice organisation.
(11) Provide minimal or no copy editing or proof reading of submissions.
(12) Publish papers that are not academic at all, e.g. essays by lay people, polemical editorials, or pseudo-science.
(13) Have a 'contact us' page that only includes a web form or an email address, and the publisher hides or does not reveal its location.
(14) The publisher publishes journals that are excessively broad (e.g. Journal of Education) or combine two or more fields not normally treated together (e.g. International Journal of Business, Humanities and Technology) in order to attract more articles and gain more revenue from author fees.

3.20.2 UGC Approved Journals

Journals are the medium through which candidates publish their articles. These sources are made available through the UGC.

UGC Approved Journals list has been replaced by UGC-CARE list so, you must have the knowledge about UG-CARE list to get the Journals.

3.20.3 UGC-CARE

UGC has set up a Consortium for Academic and Research Ethics (CARE) to ensure prevention of academic misconduct that includes plagiarism in academic writing among students, faculty, researchers, and staff.

The CARE has been set up to identify, continuously monitor and maintain "UGC-CARE Reference List of Quality Journals".

Reasons to Set up UGC-CARE

- To promote only quality research, academic integrity and publication ethics in all Indian Universities.
- For promoting high-quality publications in reputed journals to achieve higher global ranks.
- To prevent publications in dubious/predatory/sub-standard journals that reflect adversely and tarnish the Indian academia image.
- To maintain the UGC-CARE Reference List of Quality Journals for all academic purposes.

3.20.4 UGC-CARE List

The UGC-CARE list comprises four main groups. The journals submitted by UGC-CARE Council Members and Universities would be analysed by the UGC Cell.

Group A: Research Journals from all disciplines which are indexed in Scopus (Source List) or Web of Science (Arts and Humanities Citation Index Source Publication, Science Citation Index Expanded Source Publication, Social Science Citation Index Source Publication).

Group B: "UGC Approved List of Journals" from the previous list which is qualified as per the analysis protocols.

Group C: Recommended journals by UGC-CARE Council members from all disciplines which are qualified as per the analysis protocols.

Group D: Journals submitted by UGC-CARE Universities for all disciplines and languages which are qualified as per the analysis protocols.

3.20.5 Procedure to Visit UGC CARE List

Step 1 –	Visit the official website of UGC-CARE, i.e. https://ugccare.unipune.ac.in/site/website/index.aspx
Step 2 –	Search for the login button and click on it.
Step 3 –	Now you have to register yourself to get logged in. Submit your name, mobile number, address and email id carefully.
Step 4 –	In the very next step, you will have to create a password. You should not share it with anyone.
Step 5 –	Use your username and password for login.

3.20.6 Predatory Journals in the UGC List that Overlap with Beall's

1. Asian Pacific Journal of Tropical Disease
2. Australasian Medical Journal
3. Al Ameen Journal of Medical Sciences
4. Asian Journal of Chemistry
5. African Journal of Traditional Complementary and Alternative Medicines
6. Advances in Biomedicine and Pharmacy
7. American International Journal of Contemporary Research
8. Asia Pacific Journal of Education, Arts and Sciences
9. Asian Journal of Science and Technology
10. Bioscience Discovery
11. Bulletin of Environment, Pharmacology and Life Sciences
12. Biotechnological Research
13. Current Botany
14. European Journal of Science and Theology
15. Eduved Global Management Research
16. European Chemical Bulletin

17. Genetics and Molecular Research
18. HortFlora Research Spectrum
19. Interdisciplinary Toxicology
20. International Journal of Communication Networks and Information Security
21. International Journal of Current Research and Review
22. International Journal of Electrochemical Science
23. International Research Journal of Pharmacy
24. Indian Journal of Scientific Research
25. International Journal of Network Security
26. International Journal of Pharmaceutical and Phytopharmacological Research
27. International Journal of Pharmaceutical Research and Development
28. International Journal of Pharmaceutical Sciences and Drug Research
29. International Journal of Pharmaceutical Sciences and Research
30. International Journal of Renewable Energy Research
31. International Journal of Advanced Research and Review
32. International Journal of Scientific Research and Management Studies
33. International Journal of Advances in Engineering and Technology
34. Indian Journal of Advances in Chemical Science
35. International Research Journal of Pharmaceutical Sciences
36. International Journal of Pharmacy and Pharmaceutical Research
37. International Journal of Innovative Research in Science, Engineering and Technology

38. International Journal of Advanced Research in Electrical, Electronics and Instrumentation Engineering
39. International Journal of Innovative and Emerging Research in Engineering
40. International Journal of Research Publications in Engineering and Technology
41. International Journal of Innovations in Engineering Research and Technology
42. International Journal of Emerging Research in Management and Technology
43. International Journal of Engineering Technology and Computer Research
44. International Journal of Science and Research Methodology
45. International Journal of Emerging Trends in Science and Technology
46. Journal of Environmental Biology
47. Journal of Theoretical and Applied Information Technology
48. Journal of Physical Therapy Science
49. Journal of Applied Pharmaceutical Science
50. Journal of Clinical and Analytical Medicine
51. Journal of Materials and Environmental Science
52. Journal of Natural Products
53. Journal of Animal and Plant Sciences
54. Journal of Food, Agriculture and Environment
55. Journal of Information Management
56. Journal of Computing Technologies
57. Journal of Global Research in Computer Science
58. Journal of Physical Education Research
59. Journal of Advances in Science and Technology
60. National Journal of Community Medicine

61. Oncoscience
62. Oncotarget
63. Oriental Journal of Computer Science and Technology
64. Pharmacie Globale: International Journal of Comprehensive Pharmacy
65. Pharmacologyonline
66. Sport Science
67. Science Postprint
68. The Criterion: An International Journal in English
69. Turkish Online Journal of Educational Technology
70. World Journal of Science and Technology
71. World Journal of Pharmaceutical and Medical Research

Source: The Hindu, September 5, 2017.

4

Open Access Publishing

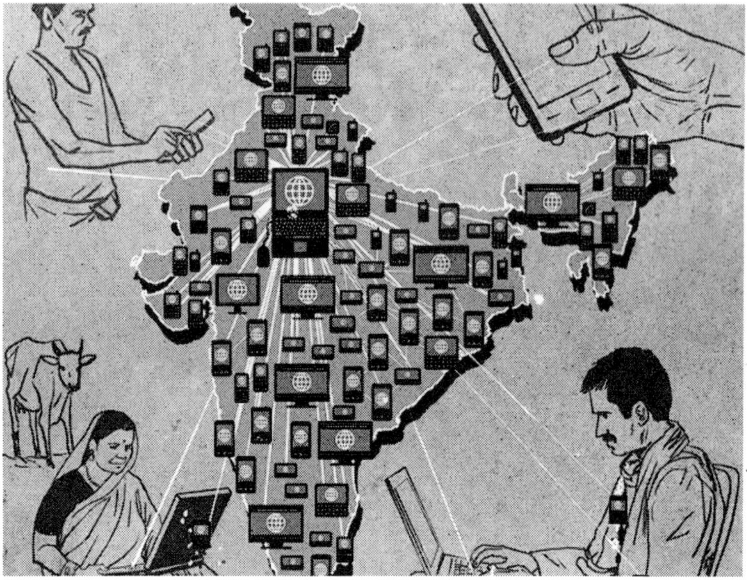

"The Last decade of Internet Evolution has been a consequence of Open access that the internet has afforded up until now."

— *Vinton Cerf*

4.1 Open Access Publications and Initiatives

Open access in the publication domain is often understood as the free online availability of the peer-reviewed and non-peer reviewed journal publications, books, conference papers and proceedings, thesis/ dissertations and monographs, to the interested along with limited restrictions in relation to the reuse. This access to the publications without any restriction is of great importance to the authors of the publications (the research gets wider reach among the scientific community), readers and future researchers (they get an idea on the recent happenings and could form a base for their research), and funders and donors (the work funded by them has greater impact by reaching a wide group of audience).

4.1.1 Naming System for Open Access

The different types of Open Access are commonly described using colour system in the current times. The most common of them are "green", "gold", and "hybrid" open access, which are described below:

(a) Gold Open Access

The publisher makes the final version of the article freely permanently accessible for everyone after the publication. The copyright for the article sits with the authors.

(b) Green Open Access

It is a system of self-archiving in which a version of the author's publication is placed in the repository freely accessible to everyone. The author mainly posts the near-final version of the manuscript after the peer-review process, the archived version of which is known as "postprint". The copyright for these publications usually lies with the publisher of, or the society affiliated with, with applicable restrictions on terms of reuse.

(c) Hybrid Open Access

These journals offer a mix of open-access and closed-access publications. This model is funded by subscriptions with open-access for only those articles for which the authors (or the funding institution) pays the publication charges.

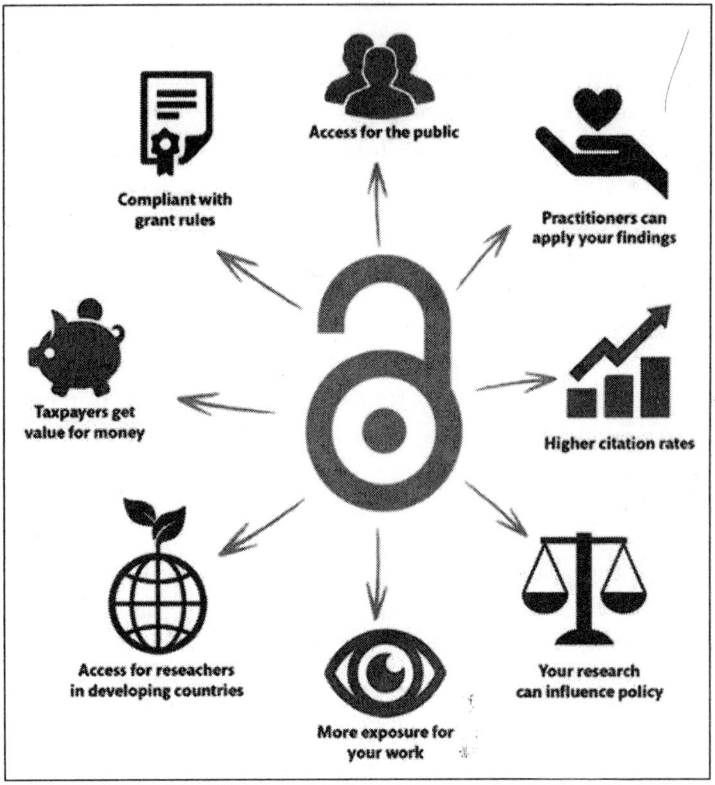

Image Courtesy: kayleighfalvey.com

4.1.2 Open Access Initiatives at the Global Level

(a) The Open Archives Initiative (OAI)

The Open Archives Initiative (OAI) is an organization which develops and applies technical interoperability standards to archives (institutional repositories) helping in the efficient dissemination of digital content. It allows people to gain access to metadata (information regarding the presence of other data). It helps improve the access to eprint achieves providing free access to scholarly communications like academic publications and journals. It makes use of Protocol for Metadata Harvesting (OAI-PMH) version 2.0 which mandates the data providers to map their data to Dublin Core (a common metadata set for open access).

The initiative is funded from the Andrew W. Mellon Foundation, Coalition for Networked Information (CNI), Digital Library Federation (DLF), National Science Foundation (NSF), the Alfred P. Sloan Foundation, and other organizations.

(b) Scholarly Publishing and Academic Resources Coalition (SPARC)

SPARC is an international coalition of over 600 academic and research institutions in the United States of America and Canada, Europe, Japan and Africa, to promote open access to scholarly articles and research data, along with the development and adoption of Open Educational Resources (OERs) in their institutions. It also collaborates with other stakeholders in the publication field like the authors, publishers, students, donors, libraries and the public to create opportunities for the dissemination of education and research.

(c) The Budapest Open Access Initiative (BOAI)

The definition of Open Access was conceptualized in a gathering of individuals at Budapest by the Open Society Institute in 2001. The recommendations developed from the leaders of Open Access movement is based on providing the public with free access and unrestricted access to scholarly research which are mostly funded out of public funds. This would enable the authors to have a wide reach to potential readers with free access and without most restrictions on copyright and licensing issues.

(d) Initiatives Undertaken by ICSU, UNESCO and CODATA

The International Council for Science (ICSU) advocates the promotion of open access by removing restrictions on reuse of academic sources with proper attribution along with an archive of the resources. The Committee on Data for Science and Technology (CODATA) is an interdisciplinary committee of the ICSU which promotes increased availability, interoperability and usability of data in research. The United Nations Educational, Scientific and Cultural Organization (UNESCO) promotes an open access of scientific information originating from public sources of fund.

4.1.3 Open Access Initiatives in India

(a) Indian Academy of Sciences

The Open access repository of publications of the Indian Academy of Sciences established in 1934 provides a platform to collect, preserve and disseminate the publications in peer-reviewed journals to a wide audience. It publishes 11 science journals reporting research work both in India and outside which are freely accessible online.

(b) The National Digital Library of India

The National Digital Library of India (NDL) is an initiative funded by the Ministry of Human Resource Development (MHRD) under its National Mission on Education through Information and Communication Technology (NMEICT) and implemented by Indian Institute of Technology, Kharagpur in 2018. It is a virtual repository of learning resources with a single-window search facility consisting of over 44 million items comprising books, thesis, articles, question papers, reports, web courses and so on.

(c) eGyanKosh

It is a national digital repository to store, index, preserve, distribute and share the digital learning resources developed by the Open and Distance Learning Institutions in the country particularly the Indira Gandhi National Open University (IGNOU). The copyright to the content available is reserved by IGNOU.

(d) Krishikosh

It is a digital repository of old and new books, journals, thesis, research publications, monographs, annual reports etc. originating from different Indian Council of Agricultural Research (ICAR) institutions and state agricultural universities (SAUs) across the country. It provides a software platform to implement all aspects of the open access policy with central integration. The repository has an exhaustive collection of over 1,60,000 articles/items which include more than 1,00,000 theses.

4.1.4 Exercises

1. Discuss the difference between free access to content and Open Access (OA).
2. Discuss the merits and demerits of Gold OA, Green OA and Hybrid OA.

4.2 SHERPA/RoMEO Online Resource to Check Publisher Copyright and Self-Archiving Policies

SHERPA RoMEO is an online resource which helps academic research community by providing information on open access policies of journals/publishers from around the world. It provides summaries of self-archiving permissions and different rights available to authors based on journals of interest. The information on the publishers is updated regularly through contributions from the community members. The SHERPA RoMEO statistics have 2562 publishers in the database from 143 countries across the globe. A total of 124 publishers from India are included in the database.

4.2.1 Archiving Policies/RoMEO Colours

The archiving policies of the journals are represented by four RoMEO Colours which are green, blue, yellow, and white. The entry from the publishers is coded according to one of these colours as shown in Table 4.1. The RoMEO Colour is applicable to the overall publications released by the publisher, that is, a publisher has to apply the "blue" archiving rights across all of their journals for obtaining a "blue" colour code. The RoMEO statistics show that out of the total number of 2562 publishers in its database, 42 per cent are in the green colour category, 33 per cent in blue, 18 per cent in white, and 7 per cent in yellow colour category.

Table 4.1: Archiving policy of journal represented by RoMEO colours

RoMEO colour	Archiving policy
Green	can archive pre-print and post-print or publisher's version/PDF
Blue	can archive post-print (i.e. final draft post-refereeing) or publisher's version/PDF
Yellow	can archive pre-print (i.e. pre-refereeing)
White	archiving not formally supported

Source: RoMEO colours. Retrieved from http://sherpa.ac.uk/romeo/definitions.php?la=en&fIDnum=|&mode=simple&version=

4.2.2 Demonstration of the Working of SHERPA RoMEO Database

Step 1: Searching on SHERPA RoMEO Database

The webpage of Sherpa/Romeo (http://sherpa.ac.uk/romeo/index.php) is browsed on the web browser and the search is performed based on the title of the specific journal as performed in Fig. 4.1 for Emerald Emerging Market Case Studies. The search could also be performed based on the title of journal, International Standard Serial Number (ISSN) of the journal or the name of the publisher.

Step 2: Interpreting the Results

The website performs the search and fetches information regarding the copyright and self-archiving policies of the journal. In case of the journal searched, i.e. "Emerald Emerging Market Case Studies", the journal falls into a RoMEO green category journal in which the author could archive the pre-print and post-print version but cannot archive the publisher's version (Fig. 4.2).

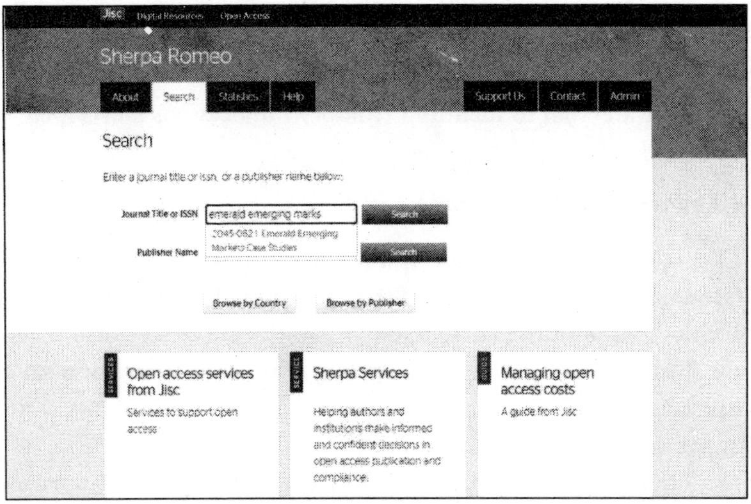

Fig. 4.1: Web interface of Sherpa/Romeo for searching the journals based on journal titles, ISSNs or Publisher Names.
Source: https://v2.sherpa.ac.uk/romeo/

Fig. 4.2: The search results for the journal providing copyright and self-archiving policies
Source: https://v2.sherpa.ac.uk/romeo/

4.2.3 Exercises

1. Select ten random journals in your discipline and perform a search on Sherpa/RoMEO online resource to examine the category of the publisher through RoMEO colour.

2. Differentiate between various national and international journals of your discipline on the basis of RoMEO colour.

4.3 Software Tool to Identify Predatory Publications Developed by SPPU

4.3.1 Predatory Publications

The consensus definition of Predatory journals according to Grudniewicz *et al.* (2019) is: "Predatory journals and publishers are entities that prioritize self-interest at the expense of scholarship and are characterized by false or misleading information, deviation from best editorial and publication practices, a lack of transparency, and/or the use of aggressive and indiscriminate solicitation practices."

These journals/publications are characterized by self-interest, usually for monetary transactions rather than making any significant contribution to the academic discipline. The main characteristics of such journals according to Tress Academic (2019) are as follows:

- The peer-review process is either absent or is not standardized.
- May not send the paper for peer-reviewing or apply any changes/editing before the publication.
- Publish a large number of low-quality papers in each issue.
- It could even publish fake or hoax papers since the quality control is quite poor leading to faulty identification.
- Send random spam emails to a group of researchers asking them for paper contributions.
- The editorial board of such journals may contain people who have never accepted to their proposal or are unaware of it.
- The name of the authors or members of the editorial board is often suspicious and falsely created.
- They may copy the website design, interface, content and advertisements of authentic and established journals.
- They may even keep names similar to the authentic and established journals to confuse the readers.
- The International Standard Serial Number (ISSN) number used by them might be inappropriate or fraudulent.

- The journal metrics used by them might be fake along with some fake names of impact factors.
- The information on the location of publisher along with other parameters might be wrong or misleading.

4.3.2 The University Grants Commission—Consortium of Academic and Research Ethics (UGC-CARE) List

The UGC-CARE reference list of quality journals is divided into two groups which are NOT hierarchic or ranked groups meaning that the names of the journal do not appear according to their position in the list or follow any order.

UGC-CARE List Group I: The journals found qualified through the protocols developed by UGC-CARE.

UGC-CARE List Group II: Journals indexed in globally recognized databases like Scopus/Web of Science etc.

The publisher of the journals can submit journal title/s through Internal Quality Assurance Cell (IQAC) of any affiliated college/University following the prescribed submission process with the recommendation of teaching faculty along with the duly signed declaration form by competent authority. The UGC-CARE list is updated quarterly, i.e. on First of January, April, July, and October (or on the next working day if there is a public holiday on these dates) every year.

The software tool to identify predatory publications developed by the University Grants Commission (UGC) cell for Journal Analysis, Centre for Publication Ethics (CPE), Savitribai Phule Pune University (SPPU), Pune, Maharashtra is demonstrated below:

Step 1: Searching for Publications on the Portal

The search for authentic and legit publications could be made with the help of an online software tool available on the website (https://ugccare.unipune.ac.in/). One needs to register on the website and search for the respective journal based on the title, ISSN, publisher, subject area or language of publication (Fig. 4.3).

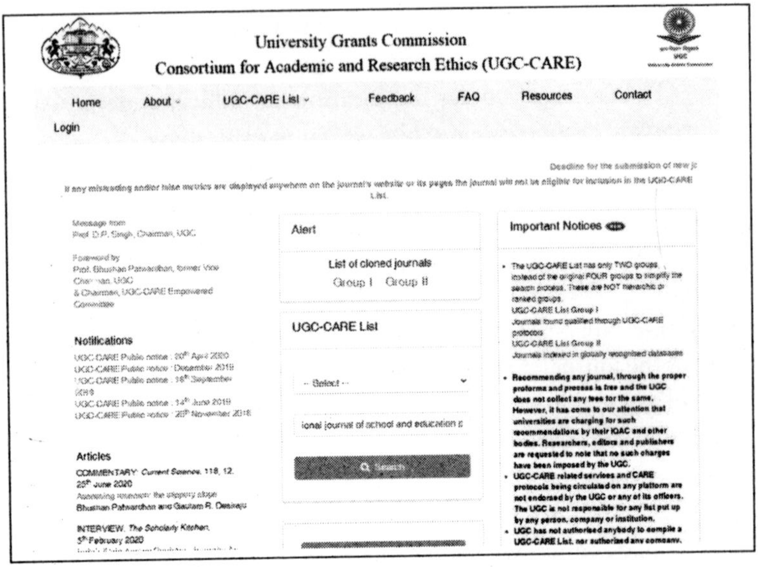

Fig. 4.3: Snapshot of the website interface allowing search of legit publications through various means.

Source: https://ugccare.unipune.ac.in/apps1/home/index

Step 2: Interpreting the Search Results

The name of the journal if available in the list of authentic publication would pop-up after performing the search function (Fig. 4.4). If the journal is not available in the database, one must check it with the two groups of the University Grants Commission—Consortium of Academic and Research Ethics (UGC-CARE) list available on the same website. The group I contains the list of journals qualified through the UGS-CARE protocols while the second list contains the journals indexed in globally recognized databases like Scopus, Web of Science etc. which will be discussed in the unit on database and research metrics. The journal not present on either of the list might be a predatory journal.

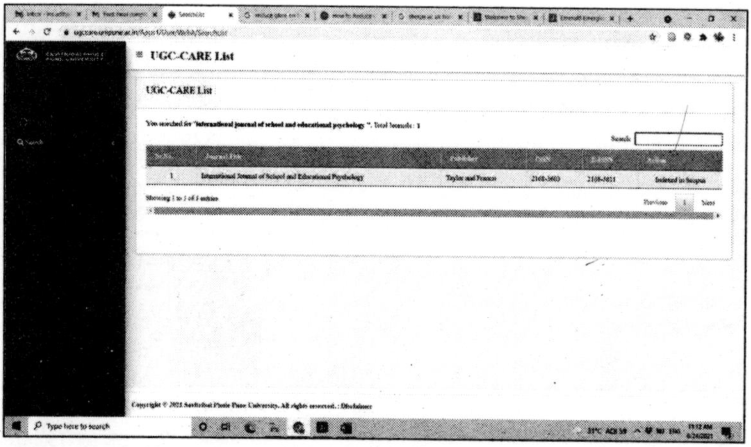

Fig. 4.4: Snapshot of the website showing the details of the publication in the UGC-CARE list

Source: https://ugccare.unipune.ac.in/apps1/home/index

4.4 Journal Finder/Journal Suggestion Tools

The journal finder/suggestion tool is an important medium to look for the suitable journal for publication of one's article. Such tool is provided by eminent publishers and organizations like Elsevier, Springer, IEEE etc. The author/searcher of the paper needs to provide the article's keywords and abstract, which is then processed by the publication website in the database to suggest the list of potential journal titles. The search results also provide information on journal metrics to understand the journal better including the impact factor of the potential journal and the ranking associated with it. The examples of some of such tools are mentioned below:

4.4.1 Journal Article Name Estimator (JANE)

Website: http://jane.biosemantics.org/

This service is offered by Biosemantics group in the Netherlands. It is mostly restricted to biomedical sciences journals. It offers the search of potential journal using article's title or abstract or just by entering the keywords in a simple search box (Fig. 4.5).

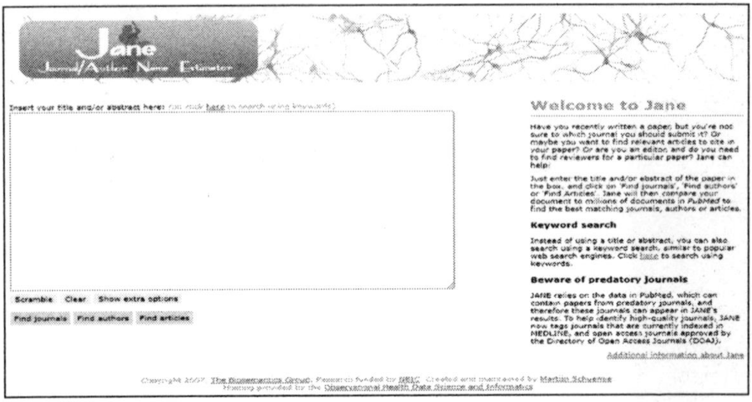

Fig. 4.5: Snapshot of the Jane tool for search of potential journals
Source: https://jane.biosemantics.org/

4.4.2 Elsevier Journal Finder

Website: https://journalfinder.elsevier.com/

The Elsevier journal finder tool provides the information on the best journals suited for the publication of research based on the title, abstract and keywords for the paper (Fig. 4.6). It also asks for the research domain from the author like life sciences, social sciences and humanities, Health etc. to suggest the best journal to match the article to Elsevier journals.

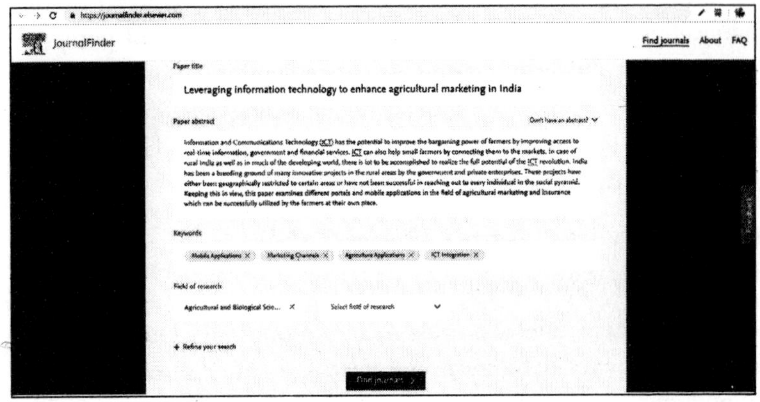

Fig. 4.6: Snapshot of the Elsevier journal finder tool for search of potential journals
Source: https://journalfinder.elsevier.com/

4.4.3 Springer Journal Suggester

Website: https://journalsuggester.springer.com/

It provides search over 2,500 journals (Springer and BioMed Central) to find the most suitable journal for the manuscript based on the title, brief text and subject area chosen by the author (Fig. 4.7).

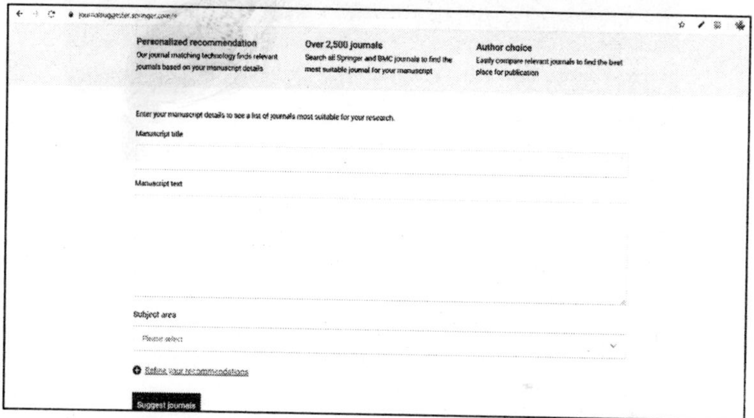

Fig. 4.7: Snapshot of the Springer journal suggester tool for search of potential journals.
Source: https://journalsuggester.springer.com/

4.4.4 IEEE Publication Recommender

Website: http://publication-recommender.ieee.org/home

The author can search the potential IEEE publication suited to his/her research from a collection of 190 periodicals and 1800 conferences organized by IEEE. The search can be made through keywords, key phrases, article title or the article itself. It also refines the search based on publication deadline which could be set by the author (Fig. 4.8).

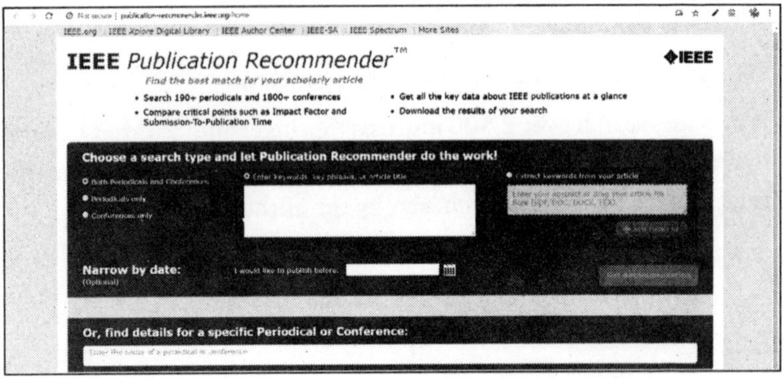

Fig. 4.8: Snapshot of the IEEE publication recommender search tool.
Source: https://publication-recommender.ieee.org/home

4.4.5 Wiley Journal Finder Tool

Website: https://journalfinder.wiley.com/

The tool is of help to the author to find the best journal in the Wiley publications group based on title and abstract of the manuscript (Fig. 4.9).

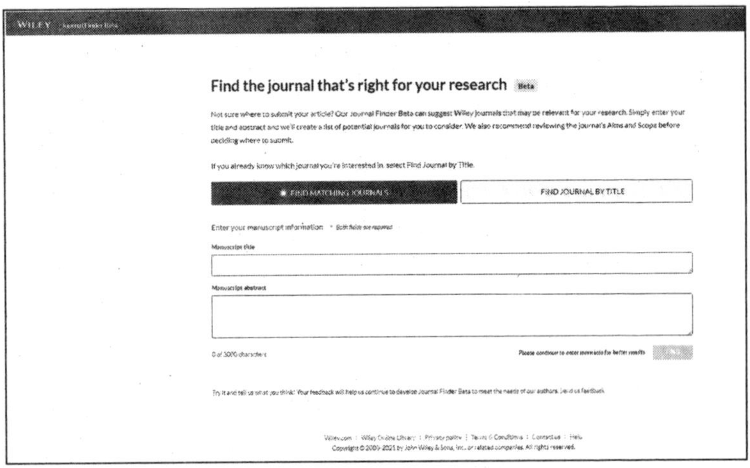

Fig. 4.9: Snapshot of the Wiley Journal Finder Tool.
Source: Website: https://journalfinder.wiley.com

4.4.6 Practical

The working of Elsevier journal finder tool is demonstrated below:

1. Conducting the Search

Website: https://journalfinder.elsevier.com/

The search is conducted by entering the title, abstract, keywords and appropriate field of research from the dropdown menu (Fig. 4.10).

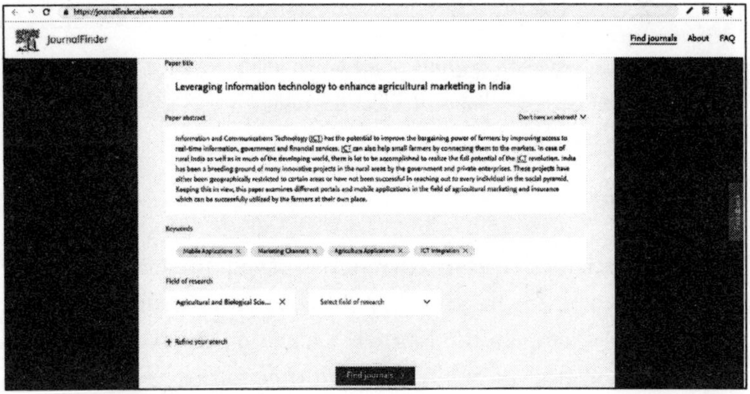

Fig. 4.10: Demonstration Snapshot of the Elsevier Journal Finder Tool with Search Inputs.

Source: Website: https://journalfinder.elsevier.com

2. *The Interpretation of the Results*

The search results show a list of 47 prospective journals matching the manuscript submitted (Fig. 4.11). The journals could be sorted on the basis of best match, journal name, citescore, impact factor, acceptance rate, time to first decision, and time to publication.

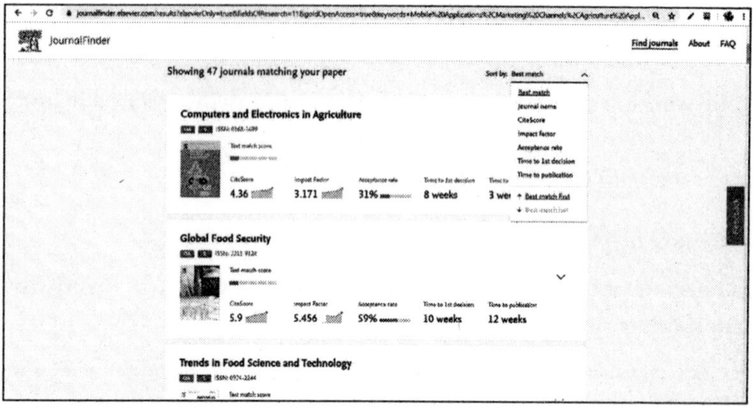

Fig. 4.11: Demonstration snapshot of the search results obtained.

Source: Website: https://journalfinder.wiley.com

4.4.7 Exercise

1. Search for the prospective journal of your research manuscript based on any three of the publishing group mentioned in the text. Compare the journals fetched on the basis of impact factor, time of publication and time to first decision on the manuscript.

5

Publication Misconduct

(Chapter Image Courtesy: Nature.com)

> **"We expect that if the research misconduct allegations are not referred for full investigations, the sabbatical request would be approved."**
>
> —*Pauline Hale*

5.0 Publication Misconduct

Misconduct is an unacceptable or inappropriate behaviour from especially a professional person. When any unlawful and improper act is done in any research work or any manuscript to be published it is considered as publication misconduct.

Publication misconduct includes plagiarism, fabrication, falsification, inappropriate authorship, duplicate submission/multiple submissions, overlapping publication, and salami publication.

5.1 Types of Publication Misconduct

5.1.1. Plagiarism

According to the Office of Research Integrity (ORI) plagiarism is the "theft or misappropriation of intellectual property and the substantial unattributed textual copying of another's work."

It is an incident of unethical adaption of another person's thoughts, ideas, data, figures, research methods, or words without giving appropriate credit, or the over-citation of another person's published work. When someone copies words, chunks of text or ideas of someone else without proper attribution then plagiarism takes place.

5.1.2. Fabrications

Fabrication is the practice of making up data or results without having performed relevant research. This concerns making up research data and/or add data, interpretations or classifications that never happened at the point of gathering data or running the experimental procedure.

5.1.3. Falsification

Falsification is the practice of changing data or results intentionally such that misleading conclusion is drawn. It refers to the practice of manipulating research data to fit a certain trend, thereby creating a false impression. This includes manipulating results and/or conclusions of a study by changing, adding or omitting data points, "inconvenient" results and images.

5.1.4. Inappropriate Authorship

Authorship is not appropriately assigned based on the author's contributions.

5.1.5. Duplicate Submission/Multiple Submissions

It refers to the practice of submitting the same manuscript or several manuscripts with minor differences (e.g., differences only in title, keywords, abstract, author order, author affiliations, or a small amount of text) to two or more journals at the same time, or submitting to another journal within an agreed or stipulated period.

5.1.6. Overlapping Publication

It refers to the practice of publishing a paper overlaps substantially with one already published.

5.1.7. Salami Publications

Salami publication refers to the practice of slicing data from a large study, could have been reported in a single paper, into different pieces and publishing them in two or more articles, all of which cover the same population, methods, and question.

5.2 Causes of Unethical Behaviour in General

Psychological traps are the main reason of all unethical behaviour. As the traps are psychological in nature, these can effectively distort the perceptions of right and wrong to a greater extent and the concerned person starts to believe his or her unethical behaviour is right. If people are not aware of these traps, they can act as illusions or webs of deception. Once the traps are identified, one can prepare for it and avoid it.

These traps can be compared with fish traps. As a fish trap is comprised a wire cage with a large funnel shaped entrance that directs the fish to swim into the cage. In the same way, sometimes an individual or organization becomes obsessed to move in an unethical direction once a psychological trap is present. Later, the action turns out to be disastrous and there are usually no simple means of reversing course.

Depending on their context, traps may be benign and can even exert a positive influence on our lives. For example, empathy is often considered the cornerstone of good ethics but in some circumstances, this personality trait can actually overpower our sense of fairness.

These impulses are reactions to internal or external stimuli. Sometimes, a stimulus is so powerful or triggers such automatic behaviour that the individual acts without recognizing that other options exist. At other times, he or she is aware of other choices, but the stimulus' impact overrides these potential actions.

There are three main categories of traps: Primary, Personality, and Defensive.

5.2.1 Primary Traps

Primary traps generally refer to external stimuli. They are the main traps that make people compelled to move in a certain direction without thinking about ethical principles. "Obedience to Authority" is a prominent type of primary traps.

Example: Most of the Students think that they must show obedience to their teachers. Later in their life, when the boss orders an employee to do something, many people quickly obey without thinking. If a person of authority orders a subordinate to do something unethical, the compelling need to obey authority serves as such a powerful external stimulus that the individual will likely obey the order without being aware of its opposition to his or her own ethical principles.

5.2.2 Personality Traps

Personality traps consist exclusively of internal stimuli in the form of various personality traits that can make people more vulnerable to wrong-doing.

An example of a personality trap is the "Need for Closure", that is, the desire or tendency to jump on the first opinion that comes to mind, rather than tolerating a state of uncertainty and taking the time to consider a problem or judgment from many different angles.

The need for closure is augmented under work conditions that make processing information more difficult, namely time pressure, fatigue, and excessive background noise. When such conditions exist, it is more difficult to tolerate a state of confusion and ambiguity.

While the need for closure is influenced by situational factors, it is also personality traits some people are more able to tolerate states of ambiguity than others.

5.2.3 Defensive Traps

Defensive traps are basically attempts to find easy ways to reverse course after any misconduct has been committed. For the most part, defensive traps are reactions to two internal stimuli: guilt and shame.

Guilt and especially shame are very painful emotions because they repeatedly question the positive view that people have within themselves. Defensive traps are insidious because they are often very successful minimizing guilt and shame. They help people deny their misconducts, thus setting them up for repeated unethical behaviour.

This type of rationalization is called "False Consensus Effect" and it is a type of defensive traps. When people do something unethical, they appease their guilt by falsely assuming that it is something everyone does, and thereby minimize their guilt feelings. He thinks "It's not that bad; it's something that happens all the time!"

5.3 Reasons of Misconduct in Research and Publication

All those psychological reasons play the key role in almost all the spheres of life while committing anything unethical or wrong. The arena of research and publication is not an exception. In this academic world these traps may or may not be so prominent but exists for sure.

Generally, we can classify these factors behind the publication and research misconducts as extrinsic factors and intrinsic factors those were mentioned earlier as external and internal stimuli.

Extrinsic factors may include some materialistic offerings like money, properties, any unjustified favour, certificates etc.

Intrinsic factors refer to the fear, affection, biasness, greed, fame, prestige, unethical mentality etc.

Sometimes, researcher or authors are directly ordered to commit an unethical action related to his or her research work or publication manuscript and the person cannot deny it. It may be due to the fear of losing something, may be due to respect for that person, may be due to exchange of some favour (monetary or others). It may be due to the publication house which has wanted the author to do so in order to gain some marketing benefits.

In some instances, the author or the researcher does some unethical actions within his work driven by his inner greed or to earn fame or any academic benefits. These acts are done even unknowingly in some cases because the academic novices are not still so much aware about these ethical issues related with research and academics.

5.4 Tactics to Handle Unethical Behaviour

A surrounding environment should be created in which psychological traps are less likely to influence the persons of that zone towards unethical behaviour. If we focus on the three types of traps that were used as examples we can find some effective tactics to get rid of them. Those traps are discussed one by one with their possible way outs.

5.4.1 Obedience to Authority

The most important thing to avoid this trap is to consult a psychologist to be a part of his or her strategy management team while being assigned with a job.

If middle managers are in a company that has a psychologist as part of its ethics team, the psychologist can help them cope with their anxiety when confronted with the trap of obedience to authority, as psychologists are well trained to mitigate intense anxiety.

5.4.2 Need for Closure

Persons with a high need for closure, for instance, are usually neither aware of having such a trait nor that it might lead them to disregard the unethical behaviour of their co-workers. If co-workers within an organization ignore or justify unethical behaviour, this supports the view of the concerned person that he or she did not do anything wrong or, if they did, that it is not that big a deal.

If that person is well known about having a high need for closure and are aware of its implications, it can be avoided being trapped.

5.4.3 False Consensus Effect

This basically sounds like: "What I (or we) did is not bad; it is something that everybody does." Once the company is aware of the false consensus effect, it is a signal that a transgression has already been committed. In such cases, established reporting and disciplinary procedures that are usually part of the company's code of business conduct and ethics should come into play.

5.5 General Tactics to Avoid Unethical Behaviour

Developing tactics to manage traps is an ongoing challenge, especially as more traps are discovered. But the fact that traps accurately define the root causes of unethical behaviour will make this task easier and the solutions more effective and efficient.

- A psychologist can help a person to cope up with the work environment keeping the ethical issues intact.
- The psychologist can also help to deal with the co-workers and to make aware of potential personality traps.
- Defensive traps should be identified without any delay to know the actions which have already been committed.
- It should also be noted that one's behaviour can be affected by more than one trap simultaneously.

5.6 Tactics to Avoid Misconduct in Academic Field

The process of making the academicians more sound in ethics should be started well advanced in their academic journey. The school students should be provided with more ethical readings specially the lessons from great personalities and their lives. Even some credit course can be effective in school and college level.

The teachers have a greater role to play. They should make the students realised with their conscience the rationale to follow an ethical life in academic field. The students will definitely be accustomed with the code of conduct and will overcome any type of trap that may come in their path in future days.

The researchers should be made well aware about the protocols and the ethical lessons about conducting a research. The impact of his research can make a great contribution to the society but any falsification can affect the society adversely too. He should be cautious about the consequences of the scientific and publication misconducts.

The author and content writers also have an immense important role in the academic world. Any kind of misleading information can produce a harmful impact in readers mind. Not only these but also the author should pay due respect to others writing while using those in his work and never should unethically use anyone's work in own name.

5.7 Conflict of Interest

> An "interest" is a commitment, obligation, duty or goal associated with a particular social role or practice.
>
> "A conflict of interest" (COI) is a situation in which a person or organization is involved in multiple interests, financial or otherwise, and serving one interest could involve working against another.

Conflict of interest occurs if, within a particular decision-making context, an individual is subject to two coexisting interests that are in direct conflict with each other. It arises when an individual finds himself or herself occupying two social roles simultaneously which generate opposing benefits or loyalties. This relates to situations in which the personal interest of an individual or organization might adversely affect a duty owed to make decisions for the benefit of a third party.

> A widely used definition is:
>
> "A conflict of interest is a set of circumstances that creates a risk that professional judgment or actions regarding a primary interest will be unduly influenced by a secondary interest."

Primary Interest refers to the principal goals of the profession or activity, such as the protection of clients, the health of patients, the integrity of research, and the duties of public officer.

Secondary Interest includes personal benefit and is not limited to only financial gain but also such motives as the desire for professional advancement, or the wish to do favours for family and friends. These secondary interests are not treated as wrong in and of them, but become objectionable when they are believed to have greater weight than the primary interests.

5.8 Conflicts of Interest in Research and Publication

Conflicts of Interest often arise in academic publishing. It can increase the possibilities of biasness that can harm the quality of research or publication. Ethical standards in academic publishing exist to avoid and deal with conflicts of interest, and the field continues to develop new rules and code of conducts. Those rules vary between journals and are not applied properly.

The issue of Conflicts of Interest is associated with research and publication agencies, sponsors, authors, journal staff, publishers, and peer reviewers.

According to the International Committee of Medical Journal Editors, "authors have a responsibility to evaluate the integrity, history, practices and reputation of the journals to which they submit manuscripts."

The avoidance of conflicts of interest and the changing of the structure of institutions to make them easier to avoid are frequently advocated for. Some institutional ethics policies ban academics from entering into specific types of COIs, for instance by prohibiting them from accepting gifts from companies connected with their work. Education in ethical COI management is also a tool for avoiding COI problems.

5.8.1 Conflict of Interest Statement for Authors

All the manuscripts sent by authors to be published as articles, research articles, editorials, reviews, book reviews, and letters that are submitted to the journal editor must be accompanied by a disclosure statement regarding conflict of interest or a declaration by the authors that they do not have any conflicts of interest to declare.

These include all financial and non-financial interests and relationships or service, whether paid or unpaid.

5.8.1.1 Financial Conflict of Interests

Any financial relationship with any organisation of any size should be disclosed, whether full-time or part-time. These may include any substantial grants from trade associations or funded by private sector firms or diversified mutual funds and investment trusts. Membership of private sector, scientific or other advisory Boards, whether paid or unpaid also should be disclosed.

In addition, any current negotiations regarding future employment or current job offers, either full- or part-time, must be disclosed.

In disclosing these financial arrangements to the editors, the authors can include dollar amounts, albeit they will not be printed in the journal. Editors may choose to exclude this information from the publication, but in no case should an editor or author consider an arrangement irrelevant based on its size alone.

5.8.1.2 Non-Financial Conflicts of Interest

Authors may have strong views about the manuscripts being submitted for publication. These may be personal or political or intellectual, and may include any expression of strongly held views relevant to the subject of submission. The authors must consider disclosing these views and the editors may choose to print any affiliations or expressions from these views that may be relevant. Such disclosures may be original or they may be references to opinions previously expressed in books or monographs, opposite editorials or public comments, or to some prior sworn testimony or lobbying of legislators or legislative bodies. Disclosable non-financial conflicts of interest will also include membership or affiliation to non-governmental organizations that have an interest in the submission.

5.9 Codes of Conduct for Publication

Journals have individual ethics policies and codes of conduct. There are also some cross-journal voluntary standards.

The Committee on Publication Ethics (COPE) publishes a code of conduct stating, "There must be clear definitions of conflicts of interest and processes for handling conflicts of interest of authors, reviewers, editors, journals and publishers, whether identified before or after publication."

The International Committee of Medical Journal Editors (ICMJE) publishes guidelines for the Conduct, Reporting, Editing, and Publication of Scholarly work in Medical Journals, and a list of journals that pledge to follow it.

The guideline lays down detailed rules for conflict-of-interest declaration by authors. It also says: "All participants in the peer-review and publication process not only authors but also peer reviewers, editors, and editorial board members of journals must consider their conflicts of interest when fulfilling their roles in the process of article review and publication and must disclose all relationships that could be viewed as potential conflicts of interest."

The Open Access Scholarly Publishers Association's Principles of Transparency and Best Practice in Scholarly Publishing is intended to separate legitimate journals from predatory publishers and defines a minimal standard; clear and clearly stated COI policies.

These recommendations have been criticized and revised to remove loopholes allowing the non-disclosure of conflicts of interest.

5.10 Criticisms of Disclosure Policies

While disclosure is widely favoured, other COI management measures have narrower support. Some publications hold the opinion that certain COIs disqualify people from certain research roles; for instance, that the testing of medicines should be done only by people who neither develop medicines nor are funded by their manufacturers.

- Those authors may feel pressured to present their research in a more biased manner to compensate.
- It may discourage beneficial academic-industrial collaboration.
- Disclosure may decrease public trust in research.
- Researchers may feel license to behave immorally.
- Some types of COI may be more likely than others to go unnoticed or unreported.
- Awareness of a COI does not make people immune to being influenced by bias.
- Disclosure discourages the judging of work purely on its merits.
- Disclosure causes more intense scrutiny for wrong doing.

5.11 Complaints and Appeals Against Publication Misconduct

Each Research journal and publication house has their own editorial policy and regulations. Those are the standards on the basis of which submitted manuscripts are verified before publication. But often some researchers and authors violate these code of conducts intentionally or unknowingly. Then any third party may lodge a complaint against that person who has committed the misconduct.

Here we have followed the appeals and complaints at the website of the Committee on Publication Ethics (COPE).

We will depict here three of those cases submitted to the COPE forum.

(Website: publicationethics.org)

Case 1: Stolen Article

Case number: 17-15

Case text (Anonymised): At acceptance but before publication, we found article A submitted to journal A was highly similar to article B, published 5 months earlier in conference proceedings in journal B by another publisher. The abstracts were nearly identical, but the author lists and affiliations did not overlap. We asked the authors to explain this and they said article A is their own work, but it was inadvertently leaked by an unnamed medical company they work with.

We told the authors of article A that in future they must declare the role of any company in their research and consider if this may be a conflict of interests. They said their article was previously submitted 4 years ago to another publisher of journal C, who rejected it. We confirmed this with the publisher, who added that their reviewers and editor are not the authors of article B.

The authors of article A said they spoke with the first author of article B, who promised to withdraw it. Article B was retracted, with the abstract being removed and a retraction notice was posted.

However, the stated reason for retraction was errors. The authors of article A said they were surprised by this.

What we know appears to be consistent with the authors of article A being the genuine authors, but the authors of article A told us the company does not want to be involved in this matter and they asked to withdraw article A, which we did. We have not contacted the authors or publisher of article B. We advised the authors of article A to contact the institutions of the authors of article B and the editor and publisher of journal B; we suggested they do not necessarily need to share details of the company because proof they are the original authors and the authors of article B are not, may be enough for an investigation. The authors of article A said they would consider this.

Question(s) for the COPE Forum

- Could we have handled this case differently?
- Should we contact the publisher of article B?
- Should we ask the institution of the authors of article A and/or article B to investigate?

Advice

The Forum was updated that there has been a further development: one of the authors of article A submitted a new article to the journal, a shorter version of which was published in the conference proceedings.

Generally, COPE recommends that authorship issues should be resolved at the institutional level. Institutions are best placed to investigate these issues, especially if there was a medical device company or drug company involved who funded the work. The institution should have a record of this involvement and they may be able to provide additional information. Also, the further misconduct of one of the authors of article A may indicate a pattern of unethical behaviour which needs to be addressed by the journal, but also by the institution.

The Forum was told that the journal plans to contact the author regarding the latest submission, and ask for an explanation. The journal also plans to contact the authors of the conference proceedings to see if they have any insight as to how a different authors group submitted the same work to the journal. After evaluating the responses, the journal may then contact the institutions of the authors of article A and possibly also the institutions of the authors of article B. The Forum agreed this was a sensible course of action.

Follow up

The authors of the latest submission and those of the conference proceeding said they had collaborated, that the conference proceeding was preliminary work, and the authors of the conference proceeding should have been acknowledged in the submission. Because of the similar issue with the previous article by the same authors, the journal still had concerns and declined to further consider the submission. The journal is asking the institutions to investigate.

Follow-up (July 2018)

The journal contacted both institutions and the other publisher. The other publisher thanked the journal for this and said they will take note of their authors' actions; neither institution has responded.

Resolution: On-going

Year: 2017

Case 2: Submission of an Already Published Case Report

Case number: 17-07

Case text (Anonymised): A case report was received at the journal. A covering letter was supplied by the two authors stating "Our work has not been published elsewhere and we have been actively involved in the preparation of the paper. No conflict of interest. Not published elsewhere. Patient consent obtained for case report and images to be published."

Originality is very highly graded in the referee's marking sheets for case reports, so the editor entered the title of the manuscript into Google, prior to sending out to referees. An exact match for the manuscript, including identical images, was found in an internet only pay per published journal.

The editor contacted the corresponding author to inform him that the journal was rejecting the article as it had already been published. The author asked if the article would be considered if the publication was withdrawn from the internet journal. The editor replied that it would not. The matter was discussed at the journal editorial board meeting and a decision taken to refer the issue to COPE.

Question(s) for the COPE Forum

- Has the journal handled the case correctly?
- Are there other actions the editor should take?

Advice

The Forum agreed that the journal had handled the case correctly and no further action is needed. The editor was correct in rejecting the paper and not considering publication if the article was withdrawn from the internet journal. The authors should be told that internet only journals are the same as printed journals, and hence the paper is considered published. The editor could consider alerting the author's institution.

Follow up: The editor thanked the Forum for their comments and considers the case closed.

Resolution: Case closed.

Year: 2017

Case 3: Author Accused of Stealing Research and Publishing Under Their Name

Case number: 16-17

Case text (Anonymised): We received a letter from a third party, accusing author A of putting his/her name against an article, published in our journal, when the research itself belongs to author A's student.

Our journal is a fully English language publication and the accusing third party and author A are from a non-English speaking country, as is the student (assumedly). The accusing third party forwarded the student's research paper to the editor which is entirely written in another language but contained an English abstract.

The Editor contacted author A and the response received included an attached confirmation letter supposedly from his/her student stating that they had no involvement in the published work by author A and that their research is completely separate to the published paper by author A.

We have several concerns:

1. It is difficult for the editor to examine the abstract the third party sent to us against the published article by author A.
2. We do not know if the response letter emailed from author A, confirming no involvement in author A's paper, is genuinely from the student.
3. The accuser's identity or relation to the matter is unknown to us. Ideally, the editor needs to contact the student directly but we need *bona fide* contact details of the student and we are not sure we would get it from the accuser or the accused author A. Google is also of little help as there are so many people with the same name.

Question(s) for the COPE Forum

- How should we go about contacting the student?
- What should be our next steps?

Advice

COPE's advice in these types of cases would be to contact the student directly. Contacting the institution in confidence through the Office of Graduate Studies would be the most normal route but some universities in some countries might not respect the confidentiality of the student. The Forum acknowledged how frustrating it must be for the journal, and that there is probably little else that can be done.

The journal could ask the third party for the contact details of the student. The only other suggestion was to see if there is a licensing board in the country that could be contacted. Any licensed professional is usually governed by a licensing board.

Follow up: The editor contacted the accuser asking for the student's details but no response has yet been received.

Follow-up (January 2017): The journal considers the case closed.

Resolution: Case Closed.

Year: 2016

(**Courtesy:** https://publicationethics.org/guidance/Case?classification=2773)

5.12 Use of Plagiarism Software Like Ithenticate and Report Interpretation

5.12.0 Plagiarism

In an instructional setting, plagiarism occurs when a writer deliberately uses someone else's language, ideas, or other original (not common-knowledge) material without acknowledging its source (Kent State University, 2014).

The definition of an act of plagiarism according to the Merriam Webster Dictionary is: "to steal and pass off ideas or words of another as one's own".

In other words, plagiarism is the process of taking ideas of other people and claiming it of their own.

The above definition applies to manuscripts, online or printed text, and to other works of the students.

5.12.1 Types of Plagiarism

5.12.1.1. Direct Plagiarism

It is the most severe form of plagiarism in which the student copies the work of others word for word. Copying the paragraph from a book or magazine and using it in the manuscript or thesis without acknowledging the source or using the text with quotation marks is an example of direct plagiarism. Such unethical act could easily be identified using software and tools like Ithenticate, Turnitin etc.

5.12.1.2. Paraphrased Plagiarism

It occurs when a few changes (minor cosmetic changes) are made to the work of some other author and is submitted as our own. It is unethical since any specific idea which falls outside the domain of common knowledge could not be included in the paper without appropriate citation.

5.12.1.3. Mosaic Plagiarism

It combines the above two forms of plagiarism in which various words, sentences, and phrases (some simply copied content, some paraphrased) are included in the manuscript without providing any acknowledgement and attributions.

5.12.1.4. Accidental Plagiarism

It is often encountered as a result of hurry and disorganized research process. In it, the citations are missing, or sources are cited incorrectly, or an idea is shared without a citation. This is also an act of plagiarism although committed accidently.

5.12.2 Demonstration of Plagiarism Software and its Interpretation

A sample article is demonstrated for plagiarism check with Ithenticate plagiarism assessment tool which compares submitted document against the internet websites and scholarly comparison database to help authors, publishers and organizations ensure that the content within the document is original and is sourced correctly. The report could be interpreted with the following steps:

Step 1: Performing a Search on Ithenticate

On registering and logging on to the ithenticate website the registration might require adequate assess from the university, if available. The student needs to enter the title of the manuscript along with his/her name (Fig. 5.1). The copy of the manuscript in a variety of formats like Microsoft word (DOC and DOCX), Word XML, plain text (TXT), Adobe PostScript, Portable Document Format (PDF), HTML, Corel WordPerfect (WPD), and Rich Text Format (RTF) could be uploaded. The file should not exceed 800 pages and 100 MB in size. The document could be submitted in 30 different languages including English.

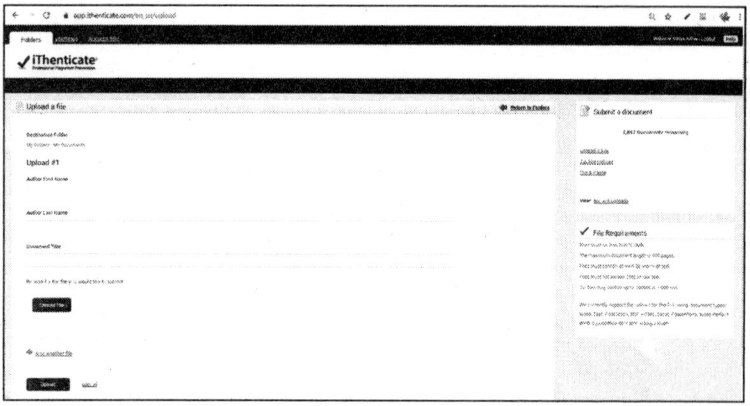

Fig. 5.1: Snapshot of Ithenticate document submission interface.

Source: Website: https://app.ithenticate.com/en_us/login

Step 2: Interpreting the Search Result

The document is processed and a page suggesting the similarity index in percentage appears. On clicking on the similarity index, the report for the particular document is generated (Fig. 5.2). The key aspects of the report are discussed below:

(a) Similarity Index: It provides a glimpse into the amount of matched content in the document in the database of ithenticate.

(b) Match overview: The highlighted text in the document is reported in different colours and is paired with the reference in the match overview section. One could see the exact source of content from which the content appears to be retrieved from the section.

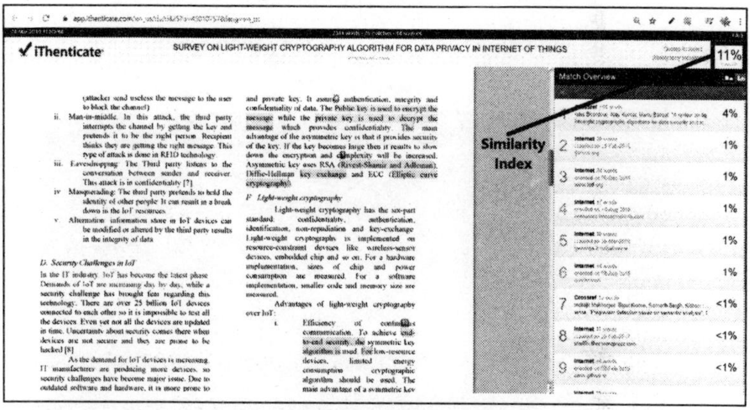

Fig. 5.2: Snapshot showing the report on the document.

Source: Website: https://app.ithenticate.com/en_us/login

Step 3: Additional Tools for Refinement of Search Results

The report could be further refined with the application of filters and settings to exclude quotes, bibliography, section of the report containing abstract, materials, methods etc. to further refine the similarity index and matched sources.

6

Database and Research Metrics

"To a Database person, every nail looks like a thumb or something like that." —*Jamie Zawinski*

6.1 Indexing Databases

6.1.1. What are Indexing Databases?

Index is a collection of items for a definite purpose. The indexing database of journals (also known as bibliographic indexes or bibliographic databases) are the collection of journals, organized by the subject, discipline, or type of publication (open access/archives).

The journals indexed in a particular database is often considered to be of greater quality than those who are not indexed. This is because for a journal to be indexed, it requires to maintain a strict set of guidelines to be included in a database of repute.

6.1.2. Importance of Indexing

The journal on being indexed in a database is easily available to other users of the same database increasing its reach. The databases differ in their indexing. Some of them index full articles while others might index only the abstract/or references associated with the articles. Indexing is quite important for a number of factors mentioned below:

- Accessibility of the journal to a wide audience of the same discipline/domain of work and expertise.
- Intermixing of high quality of information due to the presence in the same database.
- The researchers mainly start their activity with the thorough overview of the popular, well-recognized database. This results in the increased readership of journals and citations (reference of an article in other scholarly work) associated with it.

6.1.3. Demonstration

The indexing based on subject, library union catalogue, and corpora and archives is described below:

6.1.3.1 Subject Indexes

The subject indexes cover a particular subject for reaching the readers associated with it in a better way. Some of the major subject indexes are discussed below:

Agricola

It is a popular database for publications in the agricultural and allied domains like Agriculture, Animal Science, Crops, Farm Management, Horticulture, Extension and Education etc. published by the National Agricultural Library, Maryland, USA. It has an exhaustive coverage from the year 1970s to the present times.

CAB Abstracts

It provides citations and abstracts to subjects concerning applied life sciences like agriculture, veterinary sciences, forestry, rural development etc. It contains over 12.8 million bibliographic records, full-text articles, and reports with a coverage from the year 1910 produced by CAB (Commonwealth Agricultural Bureaux) International (CABI).

PubMed

It is a famous database in the field of health, medicine, life sciences, veterinary medicine, nursing, molecular biology and genetics containing over 30 million citations and abstracts for articles. It is published by the U.S. National Library of Medicine, USA.

ERIC (Educational Resources Information Center)

The ERIC database is an indexing service in the field of education and related journals, studies and reports with coverage from the year 1966.

Chemical Abstracts

It is the most comprehensive bibliographic database for scholarly research in the field of chemistry covering all important aspects of chemistry, including chemical aspects of biology and life sciences, engineering and materials science, food science, geology, medicine, physics, and polymer science. It has an exhaustive coverage starting from the year 1907.

6.1.3.2 Library Union Catalogue

WorldCat

It provides an exhaustive coverage from 12,000 libraries worldwide with millions of records for books, journal titles and materials in other formats. The coverage might be traced from 1000 A.D.—present.

COPAC (British Union Catalog)
It provides access to high-quality bibliographic information from the major libraries of the UK and Ireland.

6.1.3.3 Corpora and Archives

Early English Books Online (EEBO)

It provides full-text searchable access to the digital images of 1,50,000 books and other materials published during the 18th century. It has a coverage from 1701–1800.

American Periodicals Series Online

It contains searchable database of citations and digitized images of the pages of more than 1100 American magazines and journals published from 1741–1940s.

JSTOR

It provides full search of almost 2000 journals in more than 50 disciplines encompassing the arts, sciences, and social sciences and humanities. It functions as a not-for-profit organization established with the assistance of the Andrew W. Mellon Foundation, USA.

Exercise

1. Search for 10 research papers of your area of interest in different subject indexes. Compare the journals based on different parameters like impact factor, publication time, and place of publication.

6.2 Citation Databases

A citation database is a form of bibliographic index which makes possible to view which author have cited a publication and the number of times it has been cited. Thus, it provides an overview of citations between publications helping the user find the relationship between different publications in terms of citations.

Citation databases were developed as a means for the evaluation of publications with citation counts as a check for the user to examine the most cited publications and the authors.

The advantages and limitations of them are discussed below:

Advantages

- Helps distinguish between authors bearing the same name, or where the name of the author is presented in different ways.
- It analyzes search results by clarifying search results into multiple categories like year, name of author, source, affiliation, or categories of subject.
- Identification of most cited works in relation to a topic.
- Helps create search results in relation to the user's topic of interest.
- Alerts informing the user when his/her publication is cited in some other source.
- Compare performance of different journals in the subject area.
- Generate a user profile representing the summary and analysis of citation reports.

Limitations

- Citation count should not be considered as a fool-proof determinant of quality since there may be many other reasons responsible for the citation like negative citations, self-citations etc.
- The major focus of the citation databases is on articles published in journals. As such they might fail to cover other materials like books, conference proceedings, thesis and dissertations.

- Some of the disciplines (like science) might find better coverage than other disciplines (like humanities, arts).
- The citation database might not provide full-text access to publications which are indexed.
- Mostly in English language. Do not cover other countries and languages adequately.

The popular English language citations, namely Web of Science, Scopus and Google Scholar is discussed below:

6.2.1 Web of Science

The Web of Science is an online subscription-based citation indexing service launched in 1997 which provides access to multiple databases containing over 100 million records and over 1.4 billion cited references. The database reference cross-disciplinary research allowing comprehensive search of citations within the scientific discipline. The coverage is more in science subjects than compared to others. It provides coverage of publications from a long time period (especially regarding hard sciences dating back to 1900 to present. It is owned and maintained by Clarivate Analytics (United States).

6.2.2 Scopus

Scopus is Elsevier's collection of abstract and citation database which is currently the largest collection of peer-reviewed literature: scientific journals, books and conference proceedings. It covers research topics across fields of science, technology, medicine, social sciences, and arts and humanities with over 70 million records and 1.4 billion cited references. It also offers various smart tools and metrics to track, analyze and visualize research for conducting interdisciplinary and collaborative research. It was launched in the year 2004 by Elsevier Publishing Company, the Netherlands.

6.2.3 Google Scholar

Google Scholar was launched in the year 2004 by Google Inc., USA. It is a freely-accessible citation/bibliographic database which indexes full text or metadata of scholarly literature across various disciplines and publishing formats. The index mostly includes peer-reviewed online academic journals and books, conference papers, theses and dissertations, preprints, abstracts, technical reports, and other scholarly literature, including court opinions and patents. It is estimated to contain over 389 million documents as in January 2018 making it the world's largest academic search engine. A striking limitation of Google Scholar is the inclusion of database for even the predatory journals in its ambit.

Demonstration of Various Features of Google Scholar

Google scholar provides a free access platform for the users to make use of the wide collection of articles in its database. It is always advisable to register for free using Gmail account or institutional email account (if available on Google platform) to get the maximum from it. A typical interface of the search results retrieved by Google scholar is depicted in Fig. 6.1 with different features marked with the arrow mark.

The features of Google Scholar are discussed below:

(a) Time based search: The "Any time" search feature provides opportunity to search the articles based on year of interest. It is a very helpful feature for searching articles only from a particular period or for a definite year range.

(b) Sort by relevance/sort by date: The articles could be sorted on the basis of relevance (shows the articles which have the maximum citations) or on the basis of time (shows publications from latest to the oldest in publication year).

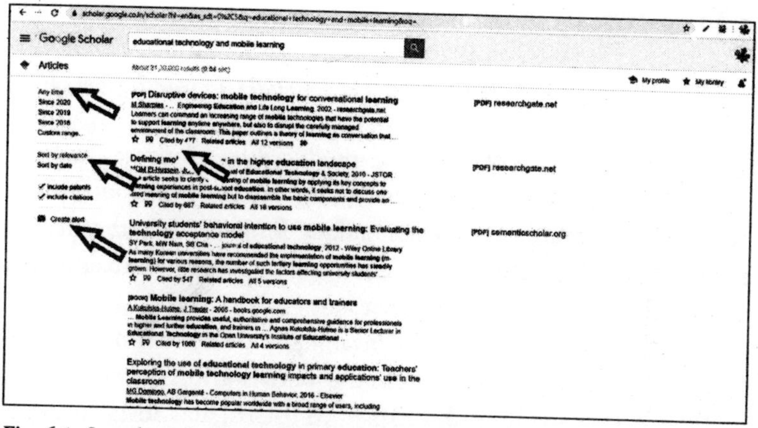

Fig. 6.1: Snapshot of a Google Scholar search result showing different features.
Source: Website: http://scholar.google.co.in

(c) **Create alert**: A particular topic/keyword of interest could be set for getting alerts in the inbox. Whenever a new publication is indexed with the same topic/keyword, an email notification is received from Google Scholar helping in providing recent developments in any area of research.

(d) **Public author profile**: On registering with Google Scholar, the user can create his profile for free and upload all of the researches on the platform. It would further help in checking on information regarding where and who is citing the publications and saving interested articles in the dedicated library of the user.

(e) **Different citation formats**: The searched article could be looked for "cite" option which shows the citation styles of the article in various formats like MLA, APA, Chicago, Harvard, and Vancouver. It also provides import options of the article in resource management software, namely BibTeX, EndNote, RefMan, and RefWorks.

(f) **Advance search options**: The platform also provides options for conducting advanced search of articles with all of the words of interest, with the exact phrase, with at least one of the words, without the words, author name, publication in a specific journal, or articles published within a set of years.

6.3 Impact Factor of Journals

6.3.1 Impact Factor of a Journal as Per Journal Citation Report (JCR)

Journal Citation Reports (JCR) as produced by Clarivate Analytics is the most used report for understanding the ranking of journals in various disciplines. JCR provides ranking for journals in the areas of science, technology, and social sciences among 12,000 journals in that field indexed in the Web of Science.

It works by aggregating the meaningful collections of citations created by researchers in most impactful journals across the world listed in the Science Citation Index Expanded (SCIE) and Social Sciences Citation Index (SSCI), part of the Web of Science Core Collection. It is both complete and editorially selective curated by a global team of experts among a collection of journals, books and conference proceedings covered in the Web of Science Core Collection to ensure accuracy in evaluating journal impact. A major limitation of JCR is that it does not cover all the journals.

Calculation of Impact Factor (IF) for a Particular Journal

The impact factor (IF) of an academic journal is a measure of the frequency with which an average article gets cited in a particular year. In other words, IF is the measure of mean number of citations per article of an academic journal in a year. It is important to measure the importance or rank of the journal by calculating the number of times the article in it are cited.

The calculation is based on a two-year period which involves dividing the number of times the articles are cited by the total number of articles which are citable in the same duration.

Calculation of 2018 IF of a Journal

A = the number of times articles published in 2016 and 2017 were cited by indexed journals during 2010.

B = the total number of "citable items" published in 2016 and 2017.

A/B = The impact factor for the year 2018.

6.3.2 Source Normalized Impact per Paper (SNIP)

SNIP was created by Professor Henk F. Moed at the Centre for Science and Technology Studies (CSTS), University of Leiden in 2009, to measure the contextual citation impact by 'normalizing' citation values. It helps in calculating the contextual citation impact by weighting citations based on the total number of citations in a subject field. It works by providing greater value to the single citation in subject areas in which citations are less likely, and *vice versa*. Thus, it helps in more accurate depiction of citation impacts providing between field comparisons. SNIP was revised in 2012 to include other indicators for measuring the impact more precisely.

6.3.3 SCImago Journal Rank (SJR)

SCImago Journal Rank (SJR indicator) is a measure of scientific influence of scholarly journals which takes both the number of citations received by a journal and the importance or prestige of the journals where such citations come from into consideration. It includes the journal and country specific indicators developed from the information contained in the Scopus database (Elsevier). SCImago's evaluation of scholarly journals is "to assign weights to bibliographic citations based on the importance of the journals that issued them, so that citations issued by more important journals will be more valuable than those issued by less important ones." (SJR indicator)

SJR allows the user to search rankings of journals, book series, conferences and proceedings, and trade journals across various subject groups across countries during different years (Fig. 6.2). It is also possible to download the data from the database.

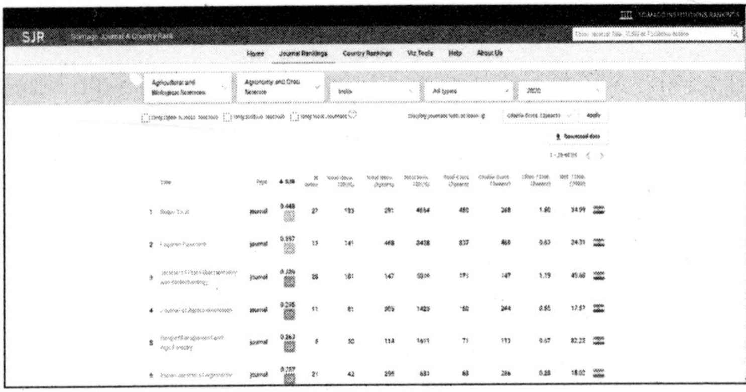

Fig. 6.2: Snapshot of SJR search for agricultural and biological sciences journals from India.

Source: Website: http:/scimagojr.com

6.3.4 The Impact Per Publication (IPP)

It was earlier known as raw impact per publication (RIP). IPP is calculated as the number of citations given in the present year to publications in the past three years divided by the total number of publications in the past three years. IPP is fairly similar to the well-known journal impact factor.

6.3.5 Cite Score

Cite Score is a ratio obtained by the number of citations a journal receives in one year to documents published in the previous three years, divided by the number of documents indexed in Scopus published in the same three years. It is similar to Impact Factor which uses a similar citation-based formula. The coverage of articles is much more in Cite Score since it covers editorials, books, conference papers etc. in addition to journal articles and uses a more transparent and reproducible metric.

6.4 Research Impact Metrics

6.4.1. h-index

h-index is a tool to measure the research output of researcher/scientist rather than the journals. The h-index is based on the total number of publications and the total number of citations to those works to provide a precise overview of an individual's research performance.

Example: If a researcher has 20 papers, each of which has at least 20 citations, their h-index is 20.

It is of use to:

- To obtain a focused overview of the researcher's performance.
- Compare different researchers with similar career length.
- To compare researchers belonging to similar field, discipline, or department who publish in the journal of the same category.

It is of limited use to:

- Compare researchers belonging to different fields, disciplines, or department.
- To assess the field, discipline, or department where there are more publications of books and conference papers since it is not adequately covered by the databases providing h-indices.

Demonstration

In the example provided below, an author has 10 papers that have been cited 66, 61, 58, 22, 18, 16, 7, 5, 4 and 2 times. This tells us that the author's h-index is 7 since this author has published at least 7 papers that have each received at least 7 citations.

Table 6.1: The article and corresponding citation numbers of a researcher

Articles	*Citation numbers*
1	66
2	61
3	58
4	22
5	18
6	16
7	**7 (h-index)**
8	5
9	4
10	2

In order to calculate the h-index manually, the articles should be organized in descending order, based on the number of times they have been cited (as shown in Table 6.1).

Points to Note

- The citation-tracking functionality in the database of Scopus, Web of Science, and Google scholar also h-index based on the content present in their database.
- Google Scholar also calculates the h-index of the author on the homepage of the citations profile feature. It is to be noted that the h-index of Google Scholar is only calculated for the publications released in the last five years. Therefore, if we see the h-index in the year 2020 than it would cover only those publications which have been published since 2015 (Fig. 6.3).
- Thus, each database may determine a different h-index for the same researcher since the content in different database is unique and may not match each other.

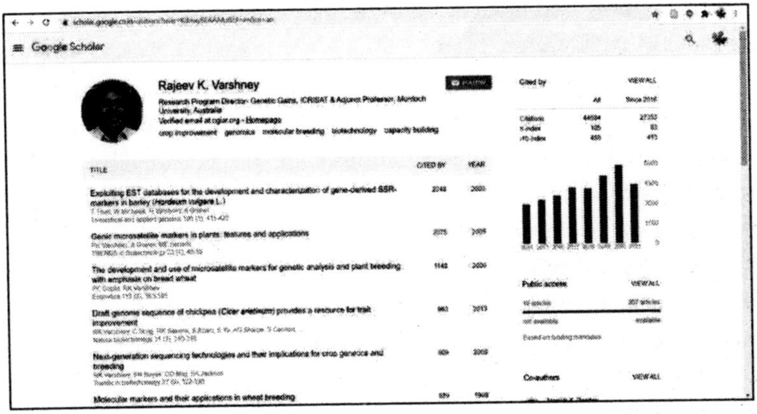

Fig. 6.3: Snapshot of Google scholar showing impact metrics of a researcher.
Source: Website: http://scholar.google.co.in/citations

6.4.2. i10 Index

The i10 index is a very simple measure used only by Google Scholar to assess the productivity of a researcher by calculating the number of publications with at least 10 citations in the last five years.

i10-Index = The number of publications with at least 10 citations.

Example: Fig. 6.3 shows that the scientist, namely Rajeev K. Varshney has an i10 index of 331 since 2015 meaning that 331 of his research articles bear at least 10 citations since the year 2015.

6.4.3. g-Index

A g-Index provides priority to the top performing articles of a researcher giving it better credit than compared to the low-cited papers.

It is calculated as "given a set of articles ranked in decreasing order of the number of citations that they received, the g-index is the unique largest number such that the top g articles received together at least g2 citations" (Leo Egghe, 2006).

The g-Index was introduced in the year 2006 and is not as widely accepted as the h-Index.

Example: A g-Index of 10 means that a researcher has published at least 10 articles that combined have received at least 100 citations. Thus, unlike the h-index these citations could be generated by only a small number of articles. For instance, a researcher with 10 papers, 5 of which have no citations with the remaining five having respectively 85, 11, 3, 2 and 1 citations would have a g-Index of 10, but a h-Index of 3 (three papers with at least 3 citations each). The g-Index looks at overall record of the researcher.

6.4.4. Altmetrics

The literal meaning of Altmetrics is "alternative metrics". It is a new measure to compliment the traditional measures of academic output of a researcher such as the number of citations, impact factor of journals and the h-index of the author.

Altmetrics score is based on locating and measuring the attention provided to research from traditional and contemporary media sources like mentions on Facebook, Twitter, or online news sites, exports of the content to citation management systems like Mendeley or Zotero, full text downloads of articles, comments and engagement in blogs or other online forums. The score rises as a greater number of people engages with the article and mentions it on the web. The source contributing to the final amount varies. For example, an article in the newspaper will count more than a tweet. The data provides useful insights on how the reports are shared and read. Thus, the Altmetrics score provides the depth of information on the reach and influence of the article and helps the researcher to know better on the audience who are going through their article.

The Altmetrics could be gathered and calculated immediately unlike the traditional measures of citation which accumulates gradually over a period of time.

References

AIAA (2007). *Publication Ethical Standards: Guidelines and Procedure.*

Hubert, Chanson (2008). *Digital Publishing, Ethics and Hydraulic Engineering: The Elusive or "Boring" Bore?* In: Stefano Pagliara 2nd International Junior Researcher and Engineer.

Gaur, R.R., Sangal R., Bagaria, (2011). *A Foundation Course in Human Values and Professional Ethics.* Excel Books.

Goleman, Daniel (2000), *Working with Emotional Intelligence,* Bantam Books, NY.

Jha, B. (2017). *Classnotes on Human Values and Ethics,* Birsa Agricultural University, Ranchi.

Joshi, M. (2018). *Human Values and Ethics,* Kalyani Publishers.

Kamble, V.B. (2015). *Classnotes on Human Values and Ethics,* College of Agriculture, Latur.

Martin, M.W. and R. Schinzinger (2005). *Ethics in Engineering,* Tata McGraw-Hill, Reprint.

Nagrajan, R.S. (2006). *Professional Ethics and Human Values.* New Age International (P) Ltd. Publishers.

National Academy of Sciences (2009). *On Being a Scientist: Third Edition.* Washington, DC: The National Academies Press. Available at: http://www.nap.edu/catalog.php?record_id=12192.

Sathya Sai Education in Human Values, *UK Newsletter,* 2/2003 www.sathyasaiehv.org.uk

Sharma, R. and Sharma, M. (2011). *Value Education and Professional Ethics.* Kanishka Publishers.

Sharma, R.A. (2011). *Human Values and Education—Axiology, Inculcation and Research.* Lall Book Depot.

Shaw, S.E., Petchey, R.P., Chapman, J., Abbott, S. (2009). "A double-edged sword? Health Research and Research Governance in UK Primary Care." *Social Science and Medicine,* 68: 912-918.

Srivastava, S. (2011). *Human Values and Professional Ethics.* S.K. Kataria and Sons.
Tripathi, A.N. (2009). *Human Values.* New Age International (P) Ltd. Publishers.
Workshop on Hydraulic Structures (IJREW'08), Pisa, Italy, Keynote, pp. 3-13, 30 July—1 August, 2008.

Websites

Google Images

www.newadvent.org
www.charactercounts.org/workplace.htm
www.iimm.org
www.iete.org
www.ti.com/corp/docs/investor/corpgov/valuesethicsconduct
www.servicelearning.org
www.pbs.org/georgewashington/classroom/civic_virtue.html
https://www.ndpublisher.in/publicationconduct.php
https://www.enago.com/academy/10-types-of-scientific-misconduct/
https://www.atlantis-press.com/policies/publishing-ethics-and-misconduct
https://gbr.pepperdine.edu/2010/08/the-root-causes-of-unethical-behaviour/
https://publicationethics.org/resources/flowcharts-new/what-do-if-you-suspect-ethical-problem
https://www.biomedcentral.com/getpublished/writing-resources/publication-ethics
https://www.slideshare.net/VishwanathAnkola/ethics-of-publication
https://publicationethics.org/resources/elearning/introduction-publication-ethics/publication-ethics-and-misconduct
https://www.hindawi.com/publish-research/authors/publication-ethics/
https://www.ncbi.nlm.nih.gov/pmc/articles/PMC5508450/

Index